High Impact at Low Decibels

High Impact at Low Decibels

How Anxiety-Filled Introverts (and others)
Can Thrive in the Workplace

Mike Schiller

BEP
BUSINESS EXPERT PRESS
Leader in applied, concise business books

High Impact at Low Decibels:
How Anxiety-Filled Introverts (and others) Can Thrive in the Workplace

First published in 2024 by
Business Expert Press, LLC
222 East 46th Street, New York, NY 10017
www.businessexpertpress.com

ISBN-13: 978-1-63742-744-6 (paperback)
ISBN-13: 978-1-63742-745-3 (e-book)

Business Expert Press Business Career Development Collection

First edition: 2025

10 9 8 7 6 5 4 3 2 1

To my family, the best family an anxiety-filled introvert could have

Description

A practical "how to" book showing the world's anxiety-filled introverts (and anxiety-filled extroverts too) how they can not only survive but also thrive in the workplace, as told by one of their own.

The workplace often seems geared toward extroverts and people with high self-confidence, and it can lead to the rest of us putting artificial limits on ourselves. In this book, you will receive **a first-hand description of how to succeed in the workplace**, as told by a self-described anxiety-filled introvert who successfully navigated that world, moving from technical roles to management to executive leadership.

This book will enable you to:

- **Better understand the internal struggles that many of us experience** and that can make life more difficult for us at work, from social anxiety to imposter syndrome to fear of public speaking and more,
- **Implement real-world, practical techniques** to mitigate these internal struggles and prevent them from becoming career derailers, while also turning them into an advantage,
- **Create your own personal toolkit** of methods for coping with stress and anxiety at work and *protect your mental health*.

This book goes beyond theory. It's not a collection of platitudes and clichéd motivational sayings–it's relatable, practical, and told with humor. If you're one of the world's many anxiety-filled introverts (or extroverts) and are looking for help thriving in the workplace, *High Impact at Low Decibels* is for you.

Contents

Testimonials

"Mike's ability to blend humor with real-world experiences makes this book a fantastic read. He introduces those experiences through a 'wish, reality, mitigation' concept, allowing readers to easily connect with the situations and gain valuable tools they can take away and use in their careers."
—**David Cauthron, CTO and Co-founder, Outpave**

"High Impact at Low Decibels *is **a must-read for introverts** and those with social anxiety.* **Schiller brings a refreshing simplicity and clarity to the subject,** *sharing his personal experiences and providing practical, actionable advice for thriving in the workplace."*—**Shawn Irving, Vice President and Chief Information Security Officer, American Airlines**

*"**This book is a terrific read not only for introverts but extroverts.** It contains many pearls of wisdom and actionable advice, rich in stories and humor."*—**Ellen Barker, Board member, retired semiconductor senior executive**

*"This book gets it right! Filled with humor and great practical advice, this book desperately needed to be written and Mike is the perfect author for the topic. **Just about anyone who has worked, or is working, in Corporate America needs this book."***—**Tim Breeding, Managing Director of IT Audit, Centennial Bank**

Acknowledgments

The genesis of this book came a few years ago when I was sitting on an airplane. I was flying to India for yet another overseas work trip. I had time to think and reflect, as one does on 20+ hour flights. I was thinking about the fact that I had a lot more years behind me in my career than ahead of me. I started wondering what might be helpful for me to share with others. Sort of a "what do I wish I knew then that I know now" kind of a thing. I started putting an outline together. It turned into a talk that I've given to a variety of audiences and now into this book.

It wouldn't have happened without the help and encouragement of a lot of people. So, thank you to:

- Tim Breeding for putting the idea in my head of turning my talk into a book.
- Kirk Tryon and Subesh Ghose for taking the time to review and provide feedback on the first draft. It's a better book because of your comments and insight.
- My brother David for being the first reader of the book as it was under development and encouraging me that it was worth doing when I wasn't sure. You were my head cheerleader throughout the process and helped keep me motivated.
- Steph for always believing in me, being patient as I obsessed over this project, and being my proofreader.
- Grant and Val for being so encouraging of this project and for the feedback on the contents.
- Kate for "getting me" and being my anxiety buddy in the family.
- Alan Pickett for the hand-drawn art that's in the book. It was great reconnecting with you after all of these years.
- Barbara Crowley for helping me build my toolkit.

Thank you to Business Expert Press for the partnership and collaboration in making this book a reality. Thanks in particular go to Acquisitions

Editor Scott Isenberg, Director of Production Charlene Kronstedt, Marketing Manager Cassie Norcutt, and Collection Editor Vilma Barr.

I'm also grateful to have worked with a lot of great bosses at Texas Instruments and to have worked at a company that made room for an anxiety-filled introvert to be successful.

Finally, thanks to you for taking the time to read this book and for tolerating its borderline-narcissistic writing style. I felt like George Harrison singing "I, Me, Mine" with the number of times I said things in the first person. I really don't think I'm any big deal, which should be obvious if you read the book. I took a stab at writing this book in the third person and removing myself from it, but I felt like it lost its immediacy and a good bit of its value. I ultimately decided that the style used was the most accessible and helpful. Right or wrong, it wasn't done without a lot of thought. Either way, I hope this book has some ideas in it that will lighten your "anxiety backpack" and help you thrive in your workplace.

Introduction

The situation is dire. The starship is under attack by the alien species of the week. The captain calmly takes in the situation and develops a plan. He barks out orders to each crew member. "Communications Officer, hail that ship! Helm, raise shields! Navigation, evasive maneuver Shat-Beta-5! Engineering, I need more power! Science Officer, do something scientific and logical! Doctor, make a sarcastic comment to cut the tension and provide an everyman perspective to the situation!" After everyone finishes following his orders, they triumph (in dramatic fashion), share a light-hearted joke around the captain's chair, and chuckle as the ship heads off into space and the credits roll. Once again, the captain's leadership came through and saved the day. He knew exactly what needed to be done, methodically deployed his crew, and was supremely confident throughout the process.

That's what leadership is, right? We all know that good leaders are bold, decisive, confident, and naturally gifted with people. And they can provide an inspirational speech on demand (accompanied by dramatic, swelling music in the background to help us understand that we're being inspired).

I mean, when you think of a leader, who comes to mind? Captain Kirk? Captain America? General Organa? Nick Fury? They all seem to fit the profile.

What if instead, I suggested Eeyore? Neville Longbottom? That Sadness character from *Inside/Out*? That's crazy talk, right? Surely, none of those characters could ever be an effective leader. I mean, it's hard to see Eeyore taking control of a tense situation on the *USS Enterprise* (although I do think it's worth us all lobbying Disney and Paramount to make the long-discussed *Star Trek* / *Winnie the Pooh* crossover a reality).

But when I look at myself, I feel I have more in common with those latter characters than the "natural" leaders I mentioned earlier. I'm an extreme introvert (hello, 93 percent introvert score on Myers-Briggs), struggle with social anxiety, and have the self-esteem of that guy who gets sand kicked in his face in those old Charles Atlas comic strips. Those characteristics don't quite seem to fit the classic profile of a leader.

Yet, I somehow managed to have a successful career as an executive at a Fortune 500 company. Not only that, but I was frequently told that my greatest strength was on the "people" side of things. How did that happen? Did I somehow manage to stumble my way through decades in the corporate world, first as a technical contributor and later as a leader, without anyone discovering that I lacked the necessary skills? Maybe I zigged and zagged at the right times and just got lucky.

Or maybe, we need to redefine our assumptions about who is equipped to be successful in the workplace, whether as a formal leader or a key individual contributor. I think most of us tend to think that people who have made it to a position of success are all super-confident extroverts who have a natural way with people. They must be to have gotten to their positions, right? But as I've spoken with successful people throughout my career, I've found that there are more people like me than there are people who fit that "classic" success profile. It's just that we all feel like we need to hide that fact and instead pretend that we fit the expected profile and personality.

Bottom line: We all have our own internal struggles. The key message of this book is to not let those struggles result in your placing artificial limits on yourself. Be aware of them, figure out how to mitigate them so that they don't become derailers, and then figure out how to make them work to your advantage. Because, as we'll see, those challenges don't have to be limitations; instead, they can provide a diversity of experience and thought that help you thrive in your profession. For me, that profession was mostly as a corporate leader and executive, but the same concept applies regardless of what you do for a living. We shouldn't look at a successful person and say "that person never had to deal with what I do, so I could never achieve that." Because it's just not true.

I'm not a motivational speaker. I tend to roll my eyes when people try to motivate me with inspirational sayings. And when I see inspirational quotes on social media, I just keep on scrolling. (I think the math on that turns out to be that I therefore scroll past approximately 75 percent of social media posts). I realize that many people get value from those sorts of things, and that's great. If you're one of them, more power to you. But it's just not me. For me, it's like eating candy—I might get a quick sugar rush but there's no lasting nutritional value there. My mind always goes straight to, "great, but how do I do that thing you're trying to inspire me to do?" For example, based on an extensive 5-second Google search, I see that Lou Holtz is credited with saying, "Your talent determines what you do. Your motivation determines how much you're willing to do. Your attitude determines how well you do it."[1] Great quote. But I need to translate it into some sort of practical action or it does me no good. So, I'll forget it as soon as I move on to the next thing (well, except in the case where I randomly chose it to use as an example in my book, which means I'm likely to remember it a little longer). The quote is a fine starting point, but what's next? How do I translate it into action?

My intent here is to share in very practical terms my experiences and what has made a difference for me. Your mileage may vary. Maybe you struggle with some of the same things I do. If so, you can take these ideas and directly apply them yourself. Or if your struggles are different, my hope is that you can use the examples I provide to generate ideas for practical steps that will work for you. My greatest fear in taking this approach is that it comes across as narcissistic ("Wow, this guy wrote a whole book about himself. Thanks, random dude who no one has ever heard of or cares about."). Hopefully, the intent is clear—I'm trying to move past the theoretical and keep things practical and actionable.

Random Dude Who No One Has Ever Heard of or Cares About

Since the practical examples in this book come from personal experience, it probably makes sense for me to provide some background on myself before we proceed. But I'll do us both a favor and keep it brief.

I spent over 30 years in corporate America, all of it in the Information Technology (IT) field. My early jobs were as a programmer and then an IT auditor. By the age of 30, I had moved into management and spent the rest of my career climbing the management ladder. By the time I retired, I was a vice president at a Fortune 500 company and the company's chief information security officer.

I wrote a book on IT auditing that was published by a major publishing house. It did well enough that I was asked to update it for a second edition and then a third edition. I also spoke regularly at major conferences in front of large audiences and as a guest lecturer at various universities.

And the whole time, I was a mess of anxiety and self-doubt inside. Yet objectively, I would have to admit that I experienced success during my career. In this book, we'll discuss some of the tools and techniques that helped along the way.

What's in This Book?

We'll start by discussing a series of observations that I made during my career. Observations in this context represent things that I found to be difficult to overcome. For each observation, we'll cover three topics:

- Wish versus reality: Sometimes we want things to be one way but the reality is different. For example, I wanted to be a star baseball player but was lacking some of the necessary tools. I was close, and if I had only had the tools for throwing, fielding, speed, hitting for average, and hitting for power, I think I could have made it. I want to have superspeed so that I can be a superhero like The Flash but am held back by the laws of physics (so far). And more relevant to this book, we'll discuss that I wanted to be a great public speaker but was terrified of public speaking.
- Mitigation: In each case, we'll look at practical steps that can keep the "reality" of these situations from derailing you. The context here will be on mitigating internal struggles (such as fear of public speaking). Obviously, no amount of mitigation is going to overcome the laws of physics and allow me to become The Flash (which is why I've shifted my focus to emulating more practical heroes, such as Batman and Green Arrow).
- Turning it into a strength: Once those internal struggles have been mitigated so that they're not derailers, they can actually

be a strength. They can bring with them a diversity of thought that provides a unique and helpful perspective. For example, when I sat on leadership teams that were full of extroverts, I was able to bring the perspective of an introvert to the table as we made decisions on plans and policies that impacted our employees. Also, the experience of overcoming those challenges can provide a stronger focus on and awareness of them. And they can also put us in position to help others who might be experiencing similar issues. Despite being one of the greatest hitters of all time, Ted Williams didn't have the reputation of being a great hitting coach because he was so naturally gifted at hitting.*2 But the journeyman player who had to work hard and try every possible technique to hone his hitting skills is in position to be a great teacher as he shares what worked (and didn't work) for him. For each of the observations, we'll cover how it can become an area of strength once the potential derailers have been mitigated.

Once we've completed those observations, we'll move on to a broader discussion on methods for coping with anxiety and stress. We'll cover three areas:

- Setting boundaries and striking a balance: We can't just totally withdraw from things that are difficult for us at work. But we can create healthy boundaries and be balanced. We'll describe practical examples of what this can look like.
- Developing your toolkit of stress-relief techniques: We all need practical tools to help us deal with anxiety and stress. In this section, we'll detail a number of techniques that you can consider for your personal toolkit.

---

* Like with most things, there are two sides to the story. Per an article on Ted Williams written by Steve Walker, "Some felt he was the world's best hitting coach. Others believed his philosophies failed to work unless you possessed his unparalleled abilities."

- Owning your challenges: We'll discuss how being aware of your internal struggles isn't about wallowing in them or using them as an excuse. But that awareness makes it much more likely that you can mitigate and overcome them. And it puts you in a position to help others and others in a position to help you.

The following box provides a quick summary view of the book layout.

Part 1: A Series of Observations

- Six Observations (one per chapter), with each covering
  - Wish Versus Reality
  - Mitigation
  - Turning It into a Strength

Part 2: Coping with Stress and Anxiety

- Setting Boundaries and Striking a Balance
- Developing Your Toolkit of Stress-Relief Techniques
- Owning Your Challenges

My hope is that you will find something in this book that will aid you in intentionally focusing on things that are holding you back from fully enjoying your life and from bringing your full self to work every day.

PART 1

A Series of Observations

(Or What Did I Learn Over the Last 30+ Years?)

CHAPTER 1

Observation 1: Talking to People Is Stressful

(aka How to Succeed as an Extreme Introvert With Social Anxiety in a World Built for Extroverts)

Imagine you're in your office building, walking down the hallway to your next meeting, and you see Bob, a co-worker who you know moderately well, coming toward you from the other direction. You briefly stop for some polite small talk and chit-chat.

For me, the conversation might go something like this:

Bob: Hey Mike.

Me: Hey, how's it going? Did you do anything fun over the weekend?

Bob: Yeah, I took the kids over to Arlington to see a Rangers game.

Me: Oh yeah, I remember you mentioned that to me. How did it go?

Bob: It was great. It was a close game and we had a great time together.

Me: I'm glad to hear it. I love that ballpark. Sounds like a great time with the family. Well, I'd better run. Have a great day, Bob.

Bob: You too. See you later.

To a casual observer, this looks like the most routine and innocuous 30-second conversation ever. But for me, it's a sea of stress that I'll be dissecting and replaying in my head for the rest of the day. Because behind the scenes, my brain is overthinking every aspect of this conversation and wearing me out. It's almost like my brain is a third participant in the conversation, talking to me at the same time as Bob.

Thoughts That Are Going Through My Head During That 30-Second Conversation:

- "His name's not coming to me. Oh yeah, it's Bob. Ugh. I couldn't think of it in time. Was it obvious that I didn't use his name?"
- "I hope he doesn't think I don't know his name. Can I drop it into the conversation later so he'll know I know it or will that sound forced?"
- "Wait, did he just say he went to the Rangers game? Dang it, he told me that last week."
- "How could I not remember that? Now he probably thinks I wasn't paying attention when he told me last week."
- "What kind of person does that? What's wrong with me? I'm such an idiot."
- "Should I tell him that I remember that conversation but just forgot? No that would be making too big a deal of it."
- "He probably thinks I'm a self-centered jerk now."
- "Maybe I should go by his office tomorrow and make a comment about it so he knows I care?"
- "Why didn't I just remember it earlier? I'm such an idiot."
- "Oh no, we're done with that topic. What do I say now? I'll just say I need to go."
- "I bet that seemed awkward."
- "What is wrong with me?"

Believe it or not, this isn't exaggerated for comic effect. This is pretty much the default of what's going on in my head during and after most conversations, even ones as simple as this. But it also isn't constant. It's not what happens during every conversation. It varies based on how healthy my state of mind is, how successful I am at controlling and focusing my thoughts, and how comfortable I am with the person I'm talking to. However, this is where my brain wants to take me. When my brain does take me here, it's exhausting. And when it doesn't, it's still exhausting because I'm working so hard to stay focused and keep my brain in check. Even if I enjoy the conversation, it wears me out, and I'm ready for some alone time to recover afterward. And keep in mind, this is the result of a completely innocent, and not unpleasant, 30 seconds of small talk. It's way worse during an actual stressful and/or significant interaction.

Wish Versus Reality

Wish

I want to build relationships and connections with people. This is true despite being an extreme introvert whose default mode is to want to be alone. There are two reasons for this—one personal and one business.

First and foremost, I value and enjoy my relationships with people. Valuing people is a driving force in my life and drives my leadership style. And I know that those relationships are good for me on a personal level. I've learned that it's not good for me to just sit in my cocoon all day, every day. Having people in my life whom I can trust and who I know care about me is invaluable. Plus, it's enjoyable to spend time with people who have shared interests and a similar outlook on life. Time with close friends, where there's familiarity and a strong comfort level, is the least draining of all social interactions.

But even if I didn't value and enjoy those relationships on a personal level, the reality is that they're critical for business success. I had a peer who used to say "It's all about relationships," and he was right. None of us are successful on our own. We all need the support of others. Even if you think you're the greatest thing since Baby Yoda and are a rugged individualist, your job almost surely doesn't exist in a vacuum. There are other people and functions that you interface with and need *something* from in order to get your job done. And you're going to be more successful if those people actually want to help you instead of hoping you crash and burn because they don't like you or being neutral on you because they don't know you. You'll need someone's help at some point. It's human nature that people are more likely to make an extra effort for you if they know you and like you. And the way to get there is by building authentic relationships ("authentic" being the key word here, not a phony "I'm nice to you only when I want something from you" type of relationship).

Relationships are important not just to get your job done but also to build your career. If you're hoping to move "up" within the company (either by promotions, additional responsibilities, internal transfers, or what-have-you), someone is going to have to be willing to promote you, give you that additional responsibility, or hire you. Again, they're much more likely to do that if they have a positive relationship with you. The Baseball Hall of Fame is a good illustration of this. Induction into the Hall is considered to be baseball's highest honor and is a goal of most great players. In order to be inducted, a player needs to be elected in a vote of long-standing members of The Baseball Writers' Association of America. Many of the people casting these votes are the same media members with whom the players interacted during their playing days. One pattern that has emerged over the years is that players who were unpleasant to the media during their playing days have a harder time getting elected to the Hall. You can argue that this isn't right and that the voters should put aside their personal feelings and look purely at the players' stats, but the reality is that not everyone does so. When this happens, the impacted players are being hurt by their failure to build relationships during their careers.

We can easily see that relationships are important and why we should want to build those relationships and connections with people. But I, for one, found that it was easier said than done.

Reality

The reality for me is that interactions are stressful and can wear me down. This gets into the topic of introverts versus extroverts. When I take personality tests, I'm an **extreme** introvert.* This doesn't

---

*There are multiple personality tests to choose from. One of the most common, and the one I've personally used the most, is the Myers-Briggs Type Indicator (MBTI). You can learn more about MBTI at www.mbtionline.com. Your company might have access to this or another personality test instrument. Otherwise, many of them, including MBTI, provide options for individuals to take the test on their website (sometimes for a fee).

mean that I'm not good at or don't enjoy conversations. It means that they drain my energy. Even those comfortable conversations with close friends that I mentioned earlier are still draining; it's just a slower drain.

When I tell my dad that I'm an introvert, he never believes me and argues with me that I'm an extrovert. That's because he's operating under the "old school" definition of introvert versus extrovert, which bases it on what a person can see (external behaviors). Under that definition, someone who is good with people and at having conversations is an extrovert. Introverts are those shy individuals who can barely hold their own when interacting with others (think Bashful from *Snow White and the Seven Dwarfs* or Fluttershy from *My Little Pony*).

But the real difference between an introvert and an extrovert is where your energy comes from. An introvert gets energy from being alone. An extrovert gets energy from being around others. It's not about the ability to socialize. An introvert can have great social skills, and an extrovert can have terrible social skills.

I think we all know people who are always on the go, making plans with friends and attending social events. I have friends and family members who absolutely hate sitting at home. Those people are extroverts (and are also like unrelatable alien beings to me). They get energy from all of those outings and social interactions, and they feel drained if they're alone for too long.

Me? I could be alone with no human interaction for 2 weeks and still not feel any pull to spend time with people. Again, that doesn't mean that I don't enjoy time with friends and family. It just means that there's no end to the amount of time I can spend enjoying quiet and solitude. I guess you could say that my "default" mode or nature is to seek alone time. There was an old episode of *The Twilight Zone* where the main character, played by Burgess Meredith, just wanted to be left alone to read his books. He managed to survive the destruction of humanity and rejoiced that now he would finally have time to read his books in peace. I'm not quite that extreme, but let's just say that I didn't find it difficult to relate to that character. (Of course, in true

Twilight Zone fashion, things didn't work out so great for him in the end.)[†1]

Conversely, when I spend time with people, no matter how much I enjoy it, it drains my batteries. As a corporate executive, I generally spent all day every day in various meetings and interactions with my co-workers. That meant that I was in a constant state of being drained and, therefore, a constant state of wanting some alone time to recharge my batteries. When I had downtime, my inclination was to close my door and catch up on emails so that I could recharge. I was never going to choose to spontaneously socialize with my co-workers, ask someone to go to a last-minute lunch with me, or exercise the technique of management by walking around (also called management by wandering around or MBWA), which is an unstructured method of informally touching base with employees to build relationships, hear issues and ideas from staff, and get status updates. No matter what my intentions were, I just wasn't going to do it because I so badly needed some alone time. It's not in my nature, plus my calendar usually didn't allow for it. So just saying, "I'm going to spend more time with people," and hoping it magically happened wasn't going to work.

In addition, social anxiety is a constant companion of mine, meaning that spontaneous social events can cause a panic attack for me. If you ask me to describe the most stressful events of my career, I might mention big presentations I had to give to the Board of Directors or other senior leaders, or I might give examples of when I had to try to lead the organization through a major crisis. But if I'm being honest with you, I'm just as likely to mention the times when someone would come by my office at 11:30 am and say, "Hey, a few of us are going to lunch. Do you want to join us?" Those events were probably about equal on the stress meter for me. When someone would invite me to a last-minute lunch, my heart would start racing. I'd start sweating. My brain would lock up and go into an infinite loop of "I'm not ready to socialize. I was planning to eat lunch at my desk and recharge. But I

[†]This was from the excellent episode of *The Twilight Zone* called "Time Enough at Last." Spoiler Alert: Burgess Meredith's character survives a nuclear war and is excited to finally have time to read all of the books he wants, but then he stumbles and breaks his glasses. Poor guy.

don't want to be rude. And I like these people and want to have a good relationship with them. But I'm not ready to socialize, I was planning to eat lunch at my desk and recharge. But I don't want to be rude and so on." Basically, I went into "fight or flight" mode. Most times, I'd eventually stutter out something about already having plans, and I'd then spend the entirety of my lunchtime second-guessing myself, beating myself up, contemplating whether I should go ahead and go to the restaurant and join them late, wondering if I offended them, and making plans for how I could make it up to them. The idea of that lunch being a relaxing time alone to recharge my batteries? Gone. Instead, even though I was alone, it would be a time that drained my batteries even more as I stressed about the situation. Other times, I might force myself to accept the lunch invitation, but I would spend the entire lunch in a state of shock because I wasn't mentally prepared to socialize and I was losing that recharge time I so badly needed.

Obviously, being an extreme introvert who seeks a lot of alone time and who panics over social interactions was not super helpful in fulfilling my wish to build relationships and connections with people.

Mitigation

What did I do to mitigate that "reality" and keep it from being a derailer? Because let's be clear, there's no doubt it could have been a derailer. If I had given in to my natural inclination to maximize alone time, it would have gotten in the way of my having a successful career (going back to the previous conversation that "it's all about relation-ships"), not to mention that my career would have been less enjoyable and fulfilling without all of the close relationships I formed.

Turn Relationship-Building Into a Task

When I recognized this as a potential issue early in my career, I took stock of my strengths to see if I could leverage any of them to overcome this challenge. One of my strengths is that I'm extremely task-oriented and organized. If I say I'm going to do something, it's going to get done and it's going to get done on time. I love to-do lists, and if something is on my to-do list, it's going to be completed and checked off. If something is on my calendar, I'm going to be there. The times in my life when I've failed to deliver on a commitment, no matter how small, were all minitraumas, and I remember each one. Many years ago, I was part of a church Sunday school class where people signed up to bring donuts each week. On my assigned week to bring donuts, I forgot and showed up to class empty-handed. I was absolutely appalled that I didn't fulfill my commitment. I mean, what if someone skipped their breakfast that morning because they were counting on the donuts that I signed up to bring? How could I be so stupid and unreliable? This was serious stuff, and I had let the team down. I called the donut coordinator right after church and apologized profusely for my gaffe. That person's response was, "Um, they're just donuts. You might want to read this book called *Don't Sweat the Small Stuff*." I'm pretty sure they wanted to recommend that I seek counseling. But it's just the way my mind works. A commitment is a commitment. This is true even of commitments I make only to myself. If I put something on my to-do list, I expect myself to do it because that's the commitment I made, even if no one else is aware of it.

I realized that because I'm so structured, I could mitigate my inclination to be alone by turning relationship-building into a task.

For example, for each job I held, I would document that role's key stakeholders and important relationships by asking myself, "who are the people that are important for me to have good relationships with if I want to be successful in this role?" and making a list of those people. The list would usually include the people on the team I was managing (i.e., the people who worked for me, for lack of a better term), my peers, my boss, and internal customers/stakeholders. I would then determine the best way for building and maintaining each of those relationships and turn that into a repeatable process. For some people, I might decide that a regularly scheduled one-on-one meeting (e.g., weekly or monthly) was the best process, and I would set it up with them as a recurring meeting. For large groups where meeting one-on-one with everyone wasn't realistic, I might schedule regular roundtables with small groups. I would also put time on my calendar for MBWA (Management by

Walking Around) and plan to spend 30 to 60 minutes of my day walking around and catching up with people. Because I knew I'd never do MBWA spontaneously, I would put it on my calendar so I could know in advance that it was part of my day and be prepared for it. Bottom line, for each important relationship, I established a goal for that relationship and figured out how to meet that goal in a concrete and structured way.

I also mentioned earlier how spontaneous social events, such as being invited to lunch at the last minute, caused panic attacks. Once I decided to turn relationship-building into a task, I started scheduling lunches and other "social" activities in advance with my friends at work. That allowed me to mentally prepare for socialization and have those lunches in a way that I could enjoy. And it also helped me with those panic attacks brought on by last-minute lunch invitations. Once I started that process of getting lunches on the calendar in advance, when people asked me to have a spontaneous lunch, instead of panicking, I had a standard response: "Lunch doesn't work for me today, but can I find some time on the calendar later this week or next week?"

The fact that I had to schedule and plan these relationship-building "tasks" didn't mean that the relationships were "phony" or that I was only doing it out of a sense of obligation. Quite the opposite, it demonstrated how much I valued the relationships because they were important enough for me to want to put in the extra effort to mitigate my default nature of seeking solitude.

Create an Agenda That Includes Time for Personal Connections

While the above technique helped me get my "foot in the door" by making sure that I had time set aside for building relationships, I also had to make sure I was successful in how I used that time. I'm a very structured person. I like meetings to have an agenda, and I want to stick to that agenda. I want to use the time efficiently so that I can move on to the next thing (and so that I can get back to being alone as soon as possible). But I found that "getting down to business" as soon as a meeting started wasn't the way to go. "Hi Cathy, come in and have a seat. How are you? Yeah, yeah, that's great. Anyway, do you have those numbers I asked for?" That's a bit off-putting and certainly doesn't communicate to the person that I care about them and value them as an individual. And it's not as enjoyable for me either. Conversations are a lot more enjoyable, and less stressful, if I'm able to connect with people on a personal level and if I can have some fun. I just had to give myself permission to do so. Since I like structure, it was as simple as having a rule in my head that an unofficial and unwritten part of the agenda for any but the most formal of meetings was to spend the first few minutes talking about anything but work. If it was a one-on-one meeting with a person I already knew well, it was easy to come up with topics. Otherwise, I had my standbys (asking about their weekend, family, upcoming trips, and so on) that could get the conversation started so I could see where it took us. If it was a meeting with a small group of people, I might throw out a generic "How was everyone's weekend?" or "Did everyone see the Rangers clinch the World Series championship last night?" Only after spending those first few minutes in more personal conversation would I dive into work topics.

Stay in the Moment

Another important element of taking advantage of relationship-building time is to actually listen to people. Remember that conversation with Bob that kicked off this chapter, where I spent as much time worrying about the conversation as actually engaging in it? I've had to train my brain to slow down so that it's not running away with all of those worries and negative thoughts when I'm talking with someone. Admittedly, I still over-analyze every conversation after the fact, but during the conversation, I've trained myself to stay focused. This was more of an "awareness and effort" thing than a trick or technique. I have to remind myself during each conversation and make the decision that I'm going to stay laser-focused on what the other person is saying. When I feel myself wandering into Anxietyville or Overthinking Land, I stop the thought and force myself to just focus on the words being said by the other person. I'm not always successful, but the more I've practiced, the better I've gotten.

Turning It Into a Strength

An interesting thing happened on the way to mitigating my extreme-introvert nature and my social anxiety. Relationship building became a strength of mine. In fact, I was told that I was considered to be one of the best people-oriented leaders in our company. I was told that I was a leader that people sought to work for, specifically because of my reputation for how I treated people.

How did that happen? It seems counter-intuitive.

What I realized was that once I had mitigated these potential derailers (basically, once I figured out how to "get out of my own way"), there are ways in which the way my brain is wired helped me.

There are a few "inputs" that worked in combination:

- I care about and respect others (this is inherent in how I was raised and also part of my belief system as a Christian).
- I care what they think (although admittedly sometimes I care too much).
- I'm hypercritical of my social skills.

These inputs, when added together and once I had mitigated my tendencies that could have derailed me from building relationships with people, resulted in a few positive "outputs."

First, I'm thoughtful about, aware of, and sensitive to others' thoughts and feelings. Unlike many people, who are focused solely on pushing their own agendas and believe that their perspective is the only one that matters, my "default" is to put myself in the other person's shoes and try to understand things from their perspective. This was invaluable, especially given my profession. I spent most of my career in the IT security and auditing fields, where my job was largely to influence others. Yes, I could write the rules about how people should behave (or audit them against the existing rules), but I found that it was much more effective in the long run when people actually believed in the value of those things and that following those rules was the right thing to do. Instead of bludgeoning people with rules and shaming them for their mistakes, my nature was to bring a more collaborative and empathetic approach to the job, which I think was a large contributor to my success.

Second, my efforts, as described in the previous section, to be "in the moment" in a conversation make me a good listener. Instead of being the person who's only half paying attention because my anxiety has me too busy being in my own head, I've been told that listening is one of my strengths.

Finally, because social interactions are difficult and stressful for me, I try to make them more enjoyable by really connecting with people—finding common interests, learning about their families and background, and so on, I've found that identifying some common ground on a personal level helps reduce the stress of interactions for me. And I've also found that it makes it easier to build authentic relationships. Those connections form more quickly when you focus on getting to know the person instead of just on the work topics.

Summary and Next Steps

Talking to people is stressful, and it's exhausting, especially for those of us who are extreme introverts and/or who experience social anxiety. But relationships are important to business success and personal happiness.

Consider taking a three-step approach to honing your relationship-building skills:

1. Inventory your strengths: Determine what strengths you have that you can leverage to help overcome your tendency to maximize alone time. An example given in this chapter was leveraging the strength of being organized and task-oriented.[‡]

2. Develop and apply mitigation techniques: Once you've identified a strength you can leverage, determine *how* you can use it to ensure you're getting out of your office and spending time with

---

[‡]Maybe you already have a good understanding of your strengths, but if not, there are tools that can help you with inventorying them. Ask your company if they have access to one of those tools. One of the most common is CliftonStrengths, and their website (www.gallup.com/cliftonstrengths) provides an option for individuals to purchase access to their assessment tool.

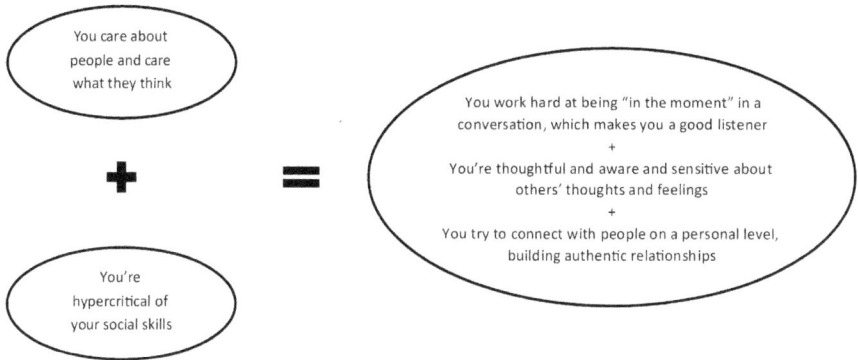

You care about people and care what they think

+

=

You work hard at being "in the moment" in a conversation, which makes you a good listener

+

You're thoughtful and aware and sensitive about others' thoughts and feelings

+

You try to connect with people on a personal level, building authentic relationships

You're hypercritical of your social skills

Figure 1.1 Example of how being an extreme introvert with social anxiety can be turned into a strength

people who are going to be important to your success. In this chapter, we discussed turning relationship-building into a task, which leveraged the strength of being organized and task-oriented.

3. Develop authentic relationships: Once you've applied mitigation techniques to ensure you're spending time with people, make sure you're leveraging that time to build authentic relationships. In this chapter, we covered techniques such as staying in the moment and creating an agenda that includes time for personal connections.

With care and focus, this can become an area of strength (see Figure 1.1 for an example). The fact that you have to be more intentional about your interactions can lead to stronger empathy, listening skills, and connections.

CHAPTER 2

Observation 2: Public Speaking Is Hard

(aka How to Overcome a Fear of Public Speaking)

Have you ever had to give a high-stakes presentation in front of a lot of people? Does anyone actually enjoy doing that? Based on extensive research, I can say with confidence that we can divide the population into two categories: people with a fear of public speaking and people who are weird. Some studies say that as much as 75 percent of the population has a fear of public speaking. If you're in the other 25 percent, I don't understand you, but congratulations and more power to you.[1]

Wish Versus Reality

Wish

Pretty early in my career, I realized that my preference was to never speak in front of an audience again for the rest of my life. **Ever.**

First and foremost, it's stressful. I generally started stressing over each presentation the day I knew it was going to happen, which means that sometimes that stress could hang over me for weeks or even months, always lurking in the back of my mind, waiting to ruin any happy moment I might be having ("You might be having fun now, but don't forget that you have that presentation coming up in a couple of weeks so don't let yourself be **too** happy").

Also, I don't feel like I'm a good extemporaneous speaker. I don't consider myself to be quick on my feet. I could prepare for what I planned to present. But questions from the audience? Terrifying.

Because you don't know what's going to be asked. My strategy was usually to try to finish my presentation right as time ended. "Oh, I'm so sorry, we don't have time for questions. I'm so disappointed because I was looking forward to your random questions that make me look like an idiot when I don't know the answer. Maybe next time."

Reality

Giving presentations was a part of my job. Avoiding them simply wasn't an option. This was a situation where I realized I had two options: either it can control me or I can control it. In other words, I could either dread it and try to avoid it (unsuccessfully) or I could embrace it and figure out how to do it well.

One time, fairly early in my career, I had to give a presentation at the end of a project. I managed to stumble through it without it turning into a disaster, but I wasn't at all happy with my performance. I felt I was tentative and that I didn't command the room. I realized that this had been a pattern for me, and I was tired of it. I resolved at that point that I was going to conquer this "public speaking" thing.

Mitigation

Making a decision that you're going to master something is great, but you then have to move into *how* you're going to do so. For me, attempting to master public speaking wasn't easy. It took hard work and intentional focus. In this section, we'll explore the various techniques I used along the way.

Practice, Practice, Practice

I realized that the key for me was preparation. I mentioned earlier that I don't think I'm a great extemporaneous speaker. I've known some people who can sound polished with little or no preparation. That's not me. If I don't take time to think through what I'm going to say and practice it, I am generally not very happy with the result.

So, I dry run every presentation. No matter what. Even if it's a topic I feel intimately familiar with. Even if it's a presentation I've given before. And if it's a new presentation, I'll probably dry run it multiple times.

My dry runs are done alone. I literally stand in an empty room and give my presentation. I would book conference rooms in my office building for those dry runs. I learned which conference rooms didn't have windows, so that people walking by wouldn't look in and think I was a crazy person talking to himself. Some people like to do dry runs in front of other people, but that doesn't work for me. I find that incredibly awkward. I need the no-stress option of being alone to work through what I want to say.

Doing these dry runs helps me figure out:

- Key points to make: How many times have you been at a presentation where the presenter basically just read their slides to you? How mind-numbing is that? I can read. If all you're going to do is read the slides to me, just send them to me and I'll read them on my own. We can skip the meeting and the presentation. I've also been in meetings where the speaker wasn't using slides but instead just looked down at the podium and read their notes word for word, never looking up at the audience. Whether I'm · using slides or speaking from notes, I'm never that guy when presenting. Because of how I prepare and practice, I rarely need to even look at the slides or my notes. I know what's on them. And I know the key messages I want to get across and what I want the audience to take away from the presentation.

- How to phrase things: Frequently, when I give a presentation for the first time, I struggle with the best way to say something. I might stumble through it and wish I had taken a different approach. I often find that things sound better in my head or on paper than when I say them out loud. The beauty of the dry run is that it lets you discover these things before you're in front of an audience. You can then adjust, try different approaches, and figure out what works best. By the time you're in front of an audience, you'll already have it all worked out, and you'll sound polished.

- How to transition from one slide (or topic) to the next: Another pet peeve of mine is when a presenter transitions to a new slide and seems to have no idea what's coming next. You see them turn their back to the audience and read the slide to remind themselves. Then, once they've recalled what the slide is, they'll turn back around and start talking again. Or when a speaker isn't using slides, they'll similarly stop talking and stare at their notes for a protracted period of time as they try to recall what their next topic or talking point is. These methods don't make for a compelling presentation. By practicing my presentation, I know what's coming next and, if using slides, can verbally transition from one slide to the next as I'm in the act of advancing the slide. This makes the presentation come across as much smoother and more cohesive.

I've taken a lot of presentation courses (something we'll discuss shortly), and one of the principles I learned is that the speaker, not the slides, is the "star" of the presentation. Too many presenters make the slides the star of the presentation. They constantly turn and look at (and read) the slides. By practicing and being prepared, I'm in a better position for the slides to be the supporting act and not the star of the show.

> **Note:** Practicing your presentation does not equal memorizing a script. No one wants to see a presenter robotically reciting memorized lines. You need to be more dynamic than that. But practicing lets you have a plan and a mental roadmap for your presentation.

Unfortunately, there will be times in your career when you're put on the spot and don't have the opportunity to dry run and practice your presentation. Years ago, I was on a trip to China with my boss and some of my peers. The first morning in the China office, we met with all of the members of the local team and presented a number of topics to them.

Two minutes before we were supposed to start, my boss came up to me and said, "Hey Mike, will you present the second topic?" My stress levels immediately skyrocketed as did my annoyance with my boss. We had this meeting on the schedule for weeks, and there was no reason why we couldn't have planned it in advance. My initial reaction (in my head) was "I haven't even seen the slides. I'm not prepared. Poor planning on your part doesn't constitute an emergency on my part. No, I don't think I will present that topic." But I knew my boss was someone who was comfortable presenting things off the cuff, and I knew he wouldn't understand or respect why I would have a problem with his request. In fact, I knew he would see it as a sign of weakness. So, after some initial grumbling, I quickly did a mental analysis and knew that "yes" was the only answer. I also knew that I couldn't step out and practice it. But I did give myself permission to mentally check out of (ignore) the first presentation of the day so that I could review the slides and work through in my head how I wanted to present my newly assigned topic. Interestingly, I found that because I had successfully practiced and delivered so many presentations in the past, the "muscles" were there for me to quickly get ready for this one, something I couldn't have done a few years earlier. After the meeting, my boss told me "You were kind of whiny about doing that presentation, but you knocked it out of the park. Good job." It was rewarding to know that my process of preparing for presentations helped me, even in an instance where I couldn't prepare. I had developed the techniques of sorting through how best to present a topic, which helped me shortcut the preparation process when I needed to.

And what about those scary questions that you might get asked during or after a presentation? You can't practice those, right? While that's true, I found it helpful to spend some time before each presentation thinking through questions that were likely to be asked and what my response to those questions would be. Over time, I became more and more adept at predicting those questions, although I was certainly still thrown some curveballs. The preparation I had done, both in practicing my presentation and in trying to identify potential questions, made me as prepared as I could possibly be, such that it was rare that I got a question I wasn't comfortable addressing. And it also put me in a position of confidence where I didn't feel bad or embarrassed when the rare occasions arose where I had to say, "That's a great question and, you know what, I'm not sure of the answer. I'll get back to you on it."

Become a Student of Presenting

Part of mastering the art of public speaking is learning as much as you can about it. I used three techniques in becoming a student of presenting.

Take Formal Training

First, I took formal training. I took a number of presentation and public speaking courses over the years. This included courses where I had to give presentations that were video-recorded, and we'd then watch the video while the instructor and my fellow students critiqued my presentation. It was uncomfortable. But I learned a lot by going through that process. It's invaluable to see yourself present and to get help from others pointing out things you could do to be more effective. By taking these classes, I learned about the physical aspects of presenting (how to use my hands, move, stand, project my voice), audience engagement (storytelling, eye contact), and how to make effective slides. Formal training "upped my game" in every aspect of being a presenter. If you work for a large company, they likely have access to public speaking training. If not, many people have had success with organizations like Toastmasters.

Observe and Learn From Other Speakers

Second, when attending presentations, I began focusing as much on the presenter's style and delivery as on the presentation content. What did the person do that I liked? This could be something physical (the way they moved and talked) or it could be how they phrased things or it could be how they engaged with the audience. I then asked myself how I could incorporate those things into my own presentation style. One of the things I learned from observing others was that the most successful speakers quickly connected with their audience, usually in a fun way. They didn't just start with "My name is Joe and today we're talking about blah blah blah." They might start with a joke or a story or some sort of audience participation. That was something I then tried to incorporate into my presentations.

Similarly, by observing the presenter, I would sometimes see them doing things that were annoying and/or distracted from their presentation. This was equally useful because I could then focus on making sure I didn't do those things. I've seen speakers that were constantly wandering back and forth around the stage or shuffling their feet with no purpose. That helped me realize the importance of being intentional with all of my movements. I've heard speakers that had a "crutch" word that they used repeatedly, to the point where I was focused more on counting how many times they used that word than on the message they were trying to convey. That helped me realize the importance of being intentional with my words and avoiding "filler" words and sounds (e.g., "um," "uh") when I'm trying to get my thoughts together.

Learn From Your Mistakes

Third, I focused on learning from my mistakes. We're all going to make mistakes when presenting and wish we had done or said things differently. But I was determined to not ever repeat a mistake, intentionally analyzing them and incorporating lessons learned into future presentations.

Years ago, we were doing a presentation to an annual meeting of our main internal customer group. My two peers and I were each supposed to present. We had 45 minutes total. The math was complex, but we eventually determined that we would each have 15 minutes to talk. I was going third. If you've ever been in that situation, you can probably predict what happened. The first two speakers went over their time allotments. By the time they were done and I got up there, we were out of time. So, what did I do? Did I shorten my presentation? No. Did I acknowledge that we were out of time and just skip doing my presentation? No. I delivered my entire presentation as planned. I mean, that's how I had practiced it. What else could I do? And I took every question from the audience. I mean, they had questions – wouldn't it be rude not to take them? But by taking this approach, I got us, and therefore the customer's meeting, even further behind.

After it was over, I felt terrible. I knew I hadn't handled it well. I went to my boss's office the next morning and asked him if my career was over. He said that it wasn't but that he was glad I asked. He then proceeded to give me some guidance and advice: "You had the opportunity to be a hero and you didn't take it. Your two peers put you in a tough spot by taking up all of your time. And everyone in that room knew they had put you in a tough spot. But instead of taking the opportunity to be a hero and keep the meeting from falling behind, you delivered your entire presentation. You tried to talk fast. That never works. And then you took every question from the audience. It's always the speaker's responsibility to control the audience and the flow of questions. You could have gotten up there and said 'We're out of time, so I'm not going to go through my slides, but here are the three key points I wanted you to take away from my presentation. I'll be available during the break and will be happy to answer any questions you might have.' You would have gotten the meeting back on track and everyone in the room would have appreciated it."[*]

This was profoundly good advice and something I used to shape my preparation process for the rest of my career. I was determined to **never** make the mistakes I made in that meeting again. If you present at many meetings, you will be in this situation, especially if you're toward the end of the agenda. People are terrible at sticking to their time slots. And it annoys everyone in the room. You **will** be put in the position where your time slot gets squeezed because the meeting is running behind. Which means you **will** have the opportunity to be a hero.

---

[*] Quote from Jim Sanders, my boss at the time, circa 2006. This was a good example of what leadership should look like. He spent no time chastising me, because he understood that there's no need to do so when you have an employee who has self-identified a mistake and is already beating himself up about it. Instead, he focused on coaching, providing actionable advice on how to improve going forward. He even had spent time looking through my pitch and identifying the key points so that he could demonstrate how I might have summarized it. As a result of this coaching, he helped me see things from a different angle and permanently changed my approach to presenting.

After this incident, I was always the guy who stuck to his time slot. If you give me 20 minutes, I'll be done in 20 minutes. If you give me 20 minutes and the meeting is running 5 minutes behind, I'll be done in 15 minutes. I'm able to do this through advance preparation. When preparing for a presentation, I think ahead of time about what I'll do if I only have 10 minutes, if I only have 5 minutes, and if I only have 1 minute. That exercise helps me really think through the key points of my presentation, which puts me in a position to be dynamic and pivot "on the fly" if the meeting is running behind.

One key to this is to have a way to see the time. You can't stick to your time if you don't know what time it is. When I get into a room where I'll be presenting, I quickly look for a clock on the wall that I can see while I'm presenting. If there isn't one, I'll put my watch on the podium or table before I start speaking. Looking at a watch on your wrist while you're presenting is distracting to the audience and isn't a good look. It makes it look like you're ready to be somewhere else. It's much less noticeable to glance down at a watch that's on a nearby surface. The same concept applies if you want to use a timer or clock on your phone. Don't pull your phone out of your pocket and look at it while you're presenting. Place your phone someplace where you can occasionally glance at it.

If you're able to master this skill of being a dynamic presenter and sticking to your time, you'll be noticed and appreciated, because not many people have that skill. It wasn't a skill I had naturally, but it was one I developed because I was determined not to repeat my mistakes. This is just one example of learning from mistakes. If you take a similar approach each time you're not happy with how things go during a presentation, you will avoid repeat incidents and over time become a more and more effective speaker.

Change Your Mindset

One of the things that can get in your way of being a successful presenter is your mindset. If you start your presentation with a mindset of dread and timidity, your audience will likely pick up on it, and you're much less likely to be successful than if you approach it with a mindset of enthusiasm and confidence.

However, changing your mindset is obviously easier said than done. So, I learned to fool myself into looking forward to it. My default mode was to stress about each presentation and think about everything that might go wrong. However, there were a couple of things that worked in my favor:

- I enjoy teaching and sharing knowledge with others.
- I enjoy having fun and using the creative side of my brain.

Public speaking gave me the opportunity to do both of those things. I just had to remind myself of that fact before each presentation.

I enjoy teaching and sharing knowledge with others: Generally, if I were speaking on a subject, it was because I had some expertise in that subject. So, I would lean into how I could use the presentation as an opportunity to share knowledge that might be of interest or use to others, because that's something I enjoy. Instead of thinking about all of the ways things could go sideways, I could get excited about sharing information with the audience. And it was also a way for me to remind myself that, as intimidating as giving the presentation might be, I knew more about the subject than most of the audience. I used to give a presentation to a subset of my company's Board of Directors on a regular basis. Each time I did it, there was a voice inside my head telling me that this was one of those "your career could be over if you screw up" meetings, which wasn't really hyperbole. But I would remind myself that I was an expert on the topic (and they weren't), meaning it was very unlikely that there was going to be a question I couldn't handle, plus it was an opportunity to share what I considered to be important information with the company's top leaders.

I enjoy having fun and using the creative side of my brain: Most presentations in the business world are humorless, soul-draining events. As someone who was on the receiving end of thousands of presentations during my career, I can state with confidence that the audience is dying for something to catch their interest. One of the best things a presenter can do is connect with their audience, especially early in the presentation.

I discovered that I enjoyed trying to find creative ways to do so, whether through stories, humor, or connecting the topic to pop culture or current headlines. It made it more fun for me and also for the audience. Of course, I had to exercise discernment. There are some presentations where either the topic or the audience lends itself to a "just the facts" model, and I needed to have the situational awareness to know what was and wasn't appropriate for any given presentation. I also had to learn what to do when that attempt at connecting with the audience didn't work. It's supremely uncomfortable to attempt a joke that doesn't land with the audience. You're hoping for laughter from the audience and instead hear crickets. But it happens. It was a learned skill to avoid discomfort in those moments, to either just move on to the next thing or to even acknowledge the failed attempt and laugh at myself in the moment, which can be another powerful way to connect with the audience.

Finding those two aspects of public speaking that I could legitimately enjoy helped me change my mindset toward those presentations and trick myself into sort of looking forward to them. You will have different things that you enjoy, but the key is to try to identify one or two things regarding the public speaking process that you legitimately enjoy and focus on them.

Take Extreme Measures

When I decided that I was going to master the skill of public speaking, it was both because it was important to my success and also because I found it to be such a stressful and miserable part of my job. One of the decisions I made was to practice a form of immersion therapy, by putting myself in the most stressful public speaking situations possible.

Specifically, I started signing up to speak at large conferences. I developed some proposals related to my field of expertise and started submitting them to various security and audit conferences. I was successful in getting them accepted, and my practice was to speak at two conferences per year, generally in front of audiences of a few hundred people. I continued this practice for a few years, until I decided I had gotten the benefit out of it that I was looking for and could stop.

This took me way out of my comfort zone but also resulted in a huge boost of confidence.

The first conference I spoke at, I was petrified before my session. I spent the morning in the bathroom because the stress was destroying my stomach. "What was I thinking???" was the phrase playing in my head on "repeat." But you know what? I was prepared, thanks to all of my practicing of the presentation, and I knew my stuff. The presentation went well, and I received great feedback on the survey from the audience. The next time I spoke at a conference, I was still pretty nervous but it was much better, because I had successfully done it before. **Experience builds confidence**. I got to the point where I'd be getting ready to speak to a room full of strangers and I was barely nervous. I would still feel some stress, as anyone with a pulse should when preparing to speak to a large audience, but it was mixed with confidence and excitement.

Again, experience builds confidence. Sometimes we have to force ourselves to get that experience, even when it's uncomfortable, so that we can build that confidence and develop those skills.

Focus on Posture and Breathing

We'll cover this in more detail in the chapter on developing your toolkit of stress-relief techniques, but I found that if I was intentional about my posture and breathing, it could have a significant impact on my confidence level when speaking.

Making myself "big" helped me feel more confident. Before I would go "on stage," I would focus on pulling my shoulders back and widening my posture. And during the presentation, I would make sure to maintain a broad stance with good posture. Think of the Superman or Wonder Woman pose that we often see (feet apart, shoulders back, hands on hips), just a bit less exaggerated (and without the hands on hips, which looks a little silly as a presenter). There's theory behind why this helps that we'll get into in that later chapter.

The other thing I would do before going on stage is focus on my breathing, taking some deep breaths and holding them for a few seconds before letting them out. I found that this helped me feel calmer and also helped me feel sharper. Again, when we cover stress-relief techniques later in the book, we'll discuss some specific breathing techniques.

Find a Friendly Face in the Audience

There's always one or more in every crowd. It seems that every audience I've ever spoken in front of, whether large or small, has someone who's giving off a positive vibe. Someone who's nodding along with what I'm saying. Someone who has an easy smile or laugh when I make an attempt at humor. Someone who just seems to be on my side. In larger audiences, there are usually multiple "good vibe" people. And God bless them, because they are incredibly encouraging to a presenter.

I've learned to identify those people early on and make sure I "check in" with them from time to time during the presentation. That doesn't mean that I stare at them and speak only to them, which would be extremely uncomfortable for them. But as a speaker, you should be making eye contact with your audience, shifting your focus throughout the presentation so that you're "addressing" each part of the audience periodically. I just make a point of making those kind and encouraging souls a regular part of my "eye contact rotation" because it gives me a boost of energy.

This concept also provides an opportunity to "pay it forward" as an audience member. I think it's important to remember that public speaking is stressful for most people, which gives us the chance to provide them a kindness by being "good vibe" people in their audience. During my time in corporate America, I attended a lot of presentations. Often, I was the senior leader in the room. I tried to always make a point of nodding my head and showing engagement during each presentation. I avoided looking at my phone and having side conversations. I consider being in the audience of a presentation to be a "golden rule" moment where I can be the sort of audience member that I hope for when I'm presenting. And when I'm attending presentations at conferences where I'm part of a large audience, I'll either try to do the same thing for the presenter if I'm sitting up front, or if I know I'm going to be multitasking and on my phone during the day and not paying full attention, I'll sit toward the back so I don't give off negative and disinterested vibes.

Turning It Into a Strength

This journey transformed me from someone who was terrified of public speaking and of giving presentations (and who was pretty mediocre at it) to an experienced and confident presenter who was told that public speaking is a strength.

The "inputs" on this journey were that:

- Presenting isn't in my natural comfort zone
- But I need and want to do it well

Based on these inputs, I made the decision to try to master the skill of public speaking. As a result:

- I've intentionally developed my presentation skills. I still have plenty of flaws, but I'm thoughtful about every aspect of public speaking because I had to learn those skills; they weren't instinctive.
- I put maximum effort into every presentation. I never mail it in. I once had a co-worker who was a naturally gifted speaker. She could always command a room and was good at presenting with very little preparation. The problem was that she knew it. She knew she could pull off a decent presentation with minimal effort. And sometimes that's exactly what she'd do. She would mail it in. She would stand up and start talking, and I could tell that she hadn't put any thought into the presentation until the moment she started speaking. She was good enough that she pulled it off and the audience (who didn't know her as well as I did) wouldn't notice. The presentation would be perfectly fine. But I knew it could have been better if she had really applied herself. That will never be me. I might give a bad presentation, but it won't be due to lack of thought or preparation.

I received consistent feedback during the back half of my career that presenting was one of my strengths, which I appreciated because I still see my flaws more than my successes, and sometimes my anxiety still gets the best of me. It's nice to hear the positive reinforcement and validation. But the success I've had doesn't come easily. I worked hard at it and continue to work hard at it, which is ultimately what it takes to be successful at things that don't come naturally. As a result, every presentation is still a significant investment of time and energy (and stress). And it's pretty inefficient, since I spend so much time in preparation for each presentation. If I'm giving a 60 minute presentation for the first time, I'm probably going to dry run it three times. That's 3 hours of practice sessions **on top of** the not-insignificant time spent developing the materials. Now, if I give that same presentation (or something similar) again, I might only dry-run it once to refresh my memory, so there are some efficiencies that can come into play. But overall, I'm not being particularly economical with my time when it comes to presentations. That's intentional. This is one area where I made the conscious choice that it was worth sacrificing efficiency to get the quality I sought. But it also meant that I needed to show discernment in accepting invitations to speak. Because of my position in my company, I received a lot of requests to speak at various department meetings. I also received invitations to speak at various external events. In the minds of the inviters, they were simply asking me to provide a 30-minute talk. In my mind, I was aware that accepting the invitation was going to be a much larger investment of time. I had to be strategic about how my time could be best spent, so I couldn't just accept every invitation. I had to consider which ones were important for me to do personally versus which ones I could delegate to a member of my team (or turn down entirely).

Summary and Next Steps

Public speaking is one of life's most anxiety-inducing experiences for a lot of us. As nice as it would be to avoid it completely, that's often simply not an option if you hope to have a successful career. That makes it important to learn how to become an effective speaker.

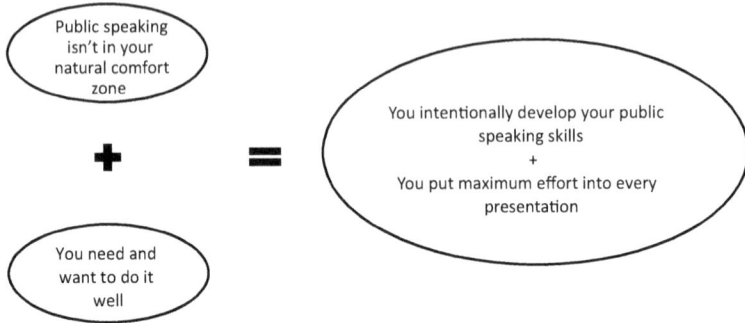

Figure 2.1 Example of how a fear of public speaking can be turned into a strength

Doing so requires a conscious decision and a plan. This chapter described techniques to help in mastering the art of public speaking, including:

- Practice, practice, practice: Prepare yourself for the presentation, such as via dry runs, so that you're comfortable with your material and approach, including knowing the key points you want to make, how you want to phrase things, and how to transition from one slide or topic to the next.
- Become a student of presenting: Take training, observe and learn from other presenters, and make a plan for how you're going to learn from and avoid repeats of your own mistakes.
- Change your mindset: Find elements of presenting that you can be excited about, and "trick" your brain into looking forward to it.
- Take extreme measures: Sign up to speak at forums, meetings, and conferences. Put yourself in uncomfortable situations so that you can develop your skills and your confidence.
- Focus on posture and breathing: Use breathing exercises to reduce stress and use "power postures" to increase confidence.
- Find a friendly face in the audience: Look for that person in the audience who you can draw positive energy from.

These are some examples of techniques that can help, but you'll need to figure out what works for you. It's different for everyone. But if you struggle with public speaking, it's not going to get better by accident. You'll need to intentionally focus on it and decide how to improve. When you do so, public speaking **is** a skill that you can develop and even master, and it can be a difference maker in your career (see Figure 2.1).

CHAPTER 3

Observation 3: Speaking in Big Meetings Is Just Another Form of Public Speaking

(aka How to Speak Up Despite a Lack of Self-Confidence)

How many times have you seen a movie with an intense conference room scene, where lots of important people are sitting around a large table discussing important things? At some point, the hero of the story will provide a key piece of information or make a critical point that changes the course of the story (and humanity). Everyone in the room will be intently focused on that hero as they share their critical insight. The hero might be super confident from the beginning and boldly make their point. Or they might stumble at the beginning but then gain momentum as they continue to talk, ultimately finishing with a flourish.

Maybe those scenes inspire you. They might make you long to be in a similar intense situation where you can save the day, while impressing everyone with your brilliance.

Me? That's one of the last places in the world I want to be. Talking to a room full of people is intimidating. If I'm in a conference room with ten, twenty, thirty, or more people who are sitting around a table and looking at me when I'm speaking, it sort of feels like I'm giving a short spontaneous presentation, but without the benefit of being able to prepare like I would if giving a planned presentation. All eyes are on me, and I feel the pressure to make a salient point that doesn't waste everyone's time.

And conference calls are even worse. At least if I'm with people in a room, I can read body language and facial expressions to get some indication as to whether what I'm saying is resonating. There will usually be some head-nodding and maybe even some "mm-hmm's" and "good points" if I'm really lucky. On a conference call, especially if there's no video, I'm just speaking into a black hole. I can't hear head nods and no one is going to give me an "mm-hmm" because they won't want to interrupt me. It's just silence. Which of course, I interpret as "Everyone thinks what I'm saying is stupid."

Wish Versus Reality

Wish

I know I have ideas and opinions to contribute when I'm in big meetings. I have skills and expertise in my field, have years of experience to draw from, have the unique perspective that my specific background and personality traits give me (a statement that's true for everyone), plus I feel like I have a pretty strong sense of "right and wrong." Put all of that together, and I usually have some thoughts to contribute to most conversations. My desire is to confidently share my inputs and add value when in those meetings.

Reality

But talking to a room full of people is intimidating. In the previous chapter, we discussed that one of my main techniques for being a successful presenter was preparation. Well, I can't prepare for "presenting" a comment that occurs to me in the midst of a conversation during a meeting.

I like to have my thoughts together before I speak. I'm not the world's fastest thinker, mainly because I like to take time to process things. So often times in meetings, while other people are peppering comments back and forth, I'll be busy formulating my thought and turning it over in my mind, looking at it from every angle and attempting to perfect it. The problem with that? By the time I feel "ready" to make my comment, the conversation has moved on. It's incredibly annoying to the rest of the room when you're the guy saying, "You know that thing we were talking about 10 minutes ago? Well, I have a thought to share on it now." The most likely response you'll receive is something along the lines of, "Uh huh. Thanks for that. Anyway, as I was saying…" When the conversation has moved on, it's moved on, and people are resistant to going back and reopening the topic. As much as I prefer to get my thoughts together before commenting, it's simply not an effective way to contribute to a meeting.

Also, because I find the whole situation stressful and intimidating, I'd really rather not speak up in the room at all. I'm much more comfortable speaking to people one-on-one. So, early in my career, I would find myself making notes of the points I'd like to make and then following up with the appropriate people after the meeting adjourned. I tried to convince myself that this was a fine way to handle things and there was no need for me to take up everyone's time by making my comment in the meeting for all to hear. But there were three problems with that approach:

- It's inefficient—There might be times when the comment I have to make really is just a niche comment that other people in the room don't need to hear. But if it's something that could substantively alter plans or decisions, I need to say it where all can hear it. There were times when I made a comment one-on-one after the meeting where the person basically said, "I wish you had said that in the room. Now we need to revisit our decision. And since we've already adjourned, I'm now going to need to follow up with everyone and maybe call us back together. Thanks a lot for wasting everyone's time, idiot." OK, they usually didn't say that last bit, but I felt like they were thinking it.

- The optics are bad—While you shouldn't make comments just so people can hear the sound of your voice, the reality is that if you want to be successful, you have to make a good impression. If I just sit silently in every meeting, it's not leaving a very good impression on people. Maybe after the meeting, I'm having some epic one-on-one conversations and making world-shatteringly great comments. But the other people in the room can't see that. They just see me as the quiet guy who might as well not even be there, since I'm adding nothing to the conversation.

- It's a cop-out for me—This is a "know thyself" thing. I have low self-confidence. Speaking to a room full of people is stressful for me. I want to find an excuse to not do it. So, I have to remind myself that my instinct to follow-up with people after the meeting is really just me trying to find an excuse to avoid speaking up.

These things worked together to interfere with my desire to add value and contribute when in meetings.

Mitigation

This is one challenge where I found that the number of practical mitigations was somewhat limited. It remained a struggle throughout my career. But it got better. There were a few areas of focus that helped.

Focus on Posture and Breathing

In the previous chapter, we discussed posture and breathing. I said that I found that if I was intentional about my posture and breathing, it could have a significant impact on my confidence level when speaking. The same techniques helped me with my confidence when speaking up in meetings with a lot of people.

Regarding posture, I described how making myself "big" helped me feel more confident and how, before I would go "on stage," I would focus on pulling my shoulders back and widening my posture. I would do the same thing in meetings. Early in my career, I would lean back in my chair during meetings, cross my legs, and not really be at what I would call a state of attention. With that approach, I often found that

I wasn't as alert as I needed to be and that it was difficult to project my voice and address the room if I had something to say. I decided to change my approach. If making myself "bigger" helped me feel more confident when presenting, could it do the same thing for me when I was seated in a meeting? So, I would focus on my posture (shoulders back, feet apart on the floor) and would sit fully upright at the table (if there was one). I found that this helped me feel more alert and less stressed and made it more natural for me to speak and address the room.

We also discussed in the previous chapter that, before going on stage, I would focus on my breathing, taking deep breaths and holding them for a few seconds before letting them out. I found that this helped me feel calmer and also helped me feel sharper. The same breathing exercises helped me in those big, stressful meetings. I would usually do a couple of cycles of breathing exercises before the meeting started and might repeat it mid-meeting if I started feeling myself getting stressed or just needing to refocus.

Again, we'll cover the posture and breathing topics in more detail in the chapter on developing your toolkit of stress-relief techniques.

Position Yourself (in the Room) for Success

Imagine you're in a conference room with about 25 people sitting around a large table. There are also chairs lining the wall, with about another 30 people occupying those chairs. At the front of the room is a speaker, presenting her slides.

> **Scenario 1:** You're sitting at the back of the room, as far away from the speaker as possible. When you make a comment or ask a question of the speaker, you can see more than 50 sets of eyes looking at you. Plus, you're having to put extra work into projecting your voice to be heard by that speaker.
>
> **Scenario 2:** You're sitting at the table at the very front of the room. The speaker is only a few feet away from you. When you make a comment or ask a question of the speaker, there might be more

than 50 sets of eyes on you, but they're behind you and you can't see them. You can almost convince yourself that you're having a one-on-one conversation with the speaker.

Which one of those two scenarios is more stressful and intimidating? For me, it's scenario 1, hands down. In that scenario, I find myself much less likely to interject comments or questions. And if I do speak, I'm much more likely to become aware of all of the eyes on me, become self-conscious, and lose focus.

Once I realized this, I started focusing on positioning myself for success in the room. I would try to get to meetings a couple of minutes early, so that I could sit toward the front. Now, everyone in the room can't use this technique or we'd all be piled on top of each other at the front of the room. But for many meetings, there are a small number of "key" attendees and decision makers. If I was one of those key attendees, I would try to sit toward the front. If I was just "one of many," I might sit more toward the middle. But I would always try to avoid sitting at the back.

The side benefit of this physical positioning was that not only was sitting closer to the front of the room less intimidating but it also helped me stay more engaged in the meeting.

Just Do It

With apologies to Nike, at some point, it's a matter of just doing it. I just needed to open my mouth and speak up.

Earlier, I mentioned that one of my struggles is that I like for my thoughts to be fully formed before I start speaking, but by then the conversation has often moved on.

The challenge I gave to myself was to start talking **before** my thoughts were perfectly formed. Once I had an idea of where I wanted to go with my comment, I started talking, trusting that I'd be able to finish forming the thought along the way.

There's a scene in *The Office* (U.S. version) where Michael Scott's boss, David Wallace, asks Michael about the key to his success.

Michael's response is a word salad that communicated nothing: "Don't ever, for any reason, do anything to anyone, for any reason, ever, no matter what, no matter where or who or who you're with or where you're going or where you've been, ever, for any reason whatsoever." Afterward, Michael shares that he'll sometimes start a sentence without knowing where it's going, hoping he'll figure it out along the way.[1]

To be clear, that's **not** what I'm recommending when I say you should challenge yourself to start talking before your thoughts are fully formed (and in fact "don't imitate Michael Scott" is pretty good advice in general). You need to have some idea of what you're trying to communicate. But I learned I didn't need to be a perfectionist. I learned that, as long as I knew the general point I wanted to make, my brain was actually capable of forming a coherent thought in real time. Maybe it wasn't perfect but it was good enough, and it let me speak up and add value to meetings versus letting the conversation pass me by while I tried to perfectly structure my comments in my head.

There's a saying that "the good is the enemy of the great,"[2] basically meaning that organizations "settle" for being adequate instead of doing the work it takes to be truly great. But I'd also say that "the perfect is the enemy of the great (or even the good)."[*] When I would try to make the perfect comment, it would slow me down to the point where I didn't contribute anything.

This is an area where practice makes "better." The more I spoke up and provided inputs that were fine even if not perfect, the better I got at it and the more confidence I had that I could continue to do so.

Have a Clear Internal Purpose

I think it's important for everyone to know what their "true north" is: to know what drives them and what their internal values and motivations are. Of course, we work to get paid. But hopefully there's more to our motivations in life than that. While I certainly don't always succeed, in

---

[*] I'm sure I'm not the first one to ever make this statement, but I came up with it out of my own brain too, so I'm not giving credit to anyone else here. Sorry, whoever said it first.

any situation, I try to ask myself, "What is the right thing to do here?" I then need to have something to guide me in answering that question (my personal guide being the value system informed by my Christian faith).

So, how does that apply to the topic of speaking up in big, stressful meetings? There are two connections.

I'm a big "there but for the grace of God" person. I knew how lucky I was to have had a good job, including everything that enabled it: the physical health and mental faculties to perform that job, parents who supported me in getting the college education I needed, and a wife who supported me throughout my career, to name just a few examples. I considered my job to be a gift, and I wanted to be a good steward of that gift. Being a good steward of that gift meant doing my job to the best of my abilities. Sitting quietly and avoiding contributing to important conversations was not "doing my job to the best of my abilities." That gave me the motivation to speak up even when it was uncomfortable.

And sometimes you'll be participating in conversations where you feel there are ethical or moral implications. While many business decisions aren't right or wrong from a moral standpoint, I've been in meetings where I felt uncomfortable with some of the proposals being discussed. Maybe I felt that the way we were planning to communicate things was misleading. Maybe I felt that proposed policies were unfair to employees. In those cases, having a strong sense of what's "right" gave me the courage to speak up even when it was uncomfortable. I couldn't **not** speak up and feel good about myself. Many years ago, I was in a meeting where we were discussing moving some jobs from one country to another. We needed the current employees to help train their replacements, which is a tough ask. As we were trying to decide how to go about approaching the current employees about it, one person in the room suggested telling them a misleading story so that they wouldn't guess what was really happening. That was a clear "right versus wrong" thing for me, and it was easy for me to speak up and suggest that we come up with a solution that met the objective while also being honest and transparent (for example, in a case like that, you can inform the employees of exactly what's happening and offer retention and milestone bonuses if they assist throughout the transition).

Now, you can't approach those sorts of situations with moral outrage or an attitude of moral superiority. All of us at times say things without considering all of the angles. Sometimes, when I spoke up on these topics, the other person would see my point and change their recommendation. Other times, they might give me additional context that helped me see it in a different light and withdraw my concern. I can't think of a case where a person said, "You're right, this is ethically wrong, but I don't care and am doing it anyway." I ran across very few mustache-twirling villains during my career. So, while having a clear moral and ethical compass should help give you motivation to speak up, it should be done in a collaborative way and with the assumption that everyone else is trying to do the right thing too.

Turning It Into a Strength

I don't think I ever became the best at contributing in those big meetings, and it continued to be a stressor for me throughout my career. But I was able to do it successfully, and the process of doing so put me in a position to actually have some related strengths:

- I was focused and intentional about my participation in meetings. I was never on auto-pilot (in fact, I guess one of the weird side benefits of being a "high anxiety" person is that we're never on auto-pilot about anything).
- I was able to strike a balance between talking too little and too much. I think we've all been in meetings with that annoying person who dominates the discussion and seems to love the sound of their own voice. There was zero risk that I was going to be that guy (no one has ever accused me of dominating a discussion). My tendency was to talk too little (or not at all), and I overcame that, putting me hopefully in the "sweet spot" of participation.

So, while I wouldn't say this was an area that became a true strength for me, I was able to mitigate it from being a derailer. As a result, there were some aspects of speaking in big meetings that actually became strengths.

Summary and Next Steps

Everyone has ideas to contribute and should have a desire to add value. But contributing in a group setting can be stressful. And if you're a perfectionist, you might want to have your thoughts fully formed before speaking, resulting in a risk of the conversation having moved on before you're ready. You might also try to convince yourself that you can just talk with people after the meeting, but that's less effective to both the discussion and your career.

Consider implementing some of the techniques described in this chapter (and/or developing your own techniques) to help you feel more confident speaking up in these "large group" settings, including:

- Focus on posture and breathing as ways to reduce stress and increase confidence.
- Position yourself (in the room) for success. Think about whether speaking up will be easier for you if you, for example, sit in the front versus the back of the room.

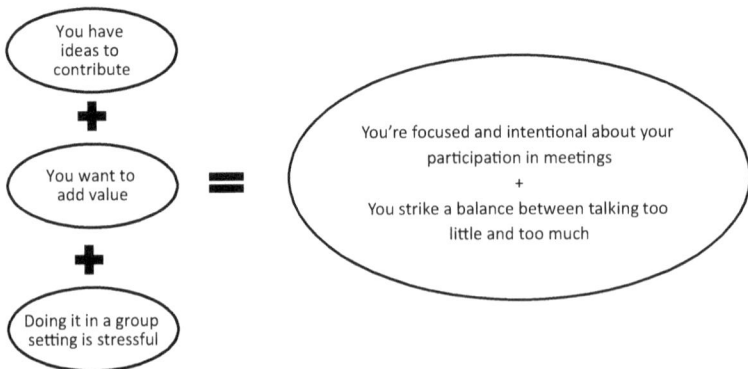

Figure 3.1 Example of how a lack of self-confidence in speaking up can be turned into a strength

- Just do it. Challenge yourself to start talking before your thoughts are perfectly formed. Once you have an idea of where you want to go with your comment, start talking and trust that you'll be able to finish forming the thought along the way. Your confidence will increase with repetition and practice.
- Have a clear internal purpose. Doing so will help give you the motivation and courage to speak up on matters that are important to you.

With focus, your participation in these meetings can shift from being a weakness to being effective, intentional, and balanced (see Figure 3.1).

CHAPTER 4

Observation 4: Change Is Hard

(aka How to Become Less Resistant to Change)

Do you want to know how much I hate change? I've eaten the same things for breakfast and lunch every day for decades.

Imagine opening your pantry and seeing an entire shelf of box after box of the same cereal. Well, I don't have to imagine it because that describes my pantry. Raisin Nut Bran cereal has been my breakfast every morning since the 90s. A while back, General Mills made a change to my cereal and removed the nuts from Raisin Nut Bran. How could they still call it Raisin **Nut** Bran if they removed the nuts you might ask? Great question. Their claim was that there was a nut coating around the raisins. Pretty weak argument, if you ask me. What was I to do? My cereal was no longer the same. Was I going to have to settle for Raisin Nutless Bran? Was I going to have to identify a new all-time cereal? I wrote General Mills a letter protesting this outrageous and unwelcome change, and I was relieved to receive a letter back informing me that they were reversing their regrettable decision and restoring the nuts to my beloved cereal. Crisis averted.

Similarly, for pretty much my entire career, at lunchtime, I would microwave a frozen pizza and eat it at my desk. This practice was well known by my co-workers. If someone wanted to talk to me around lunchtime, they wouldn't ask me if I had had lunch yet. They would ask me if I had had my pizza yet. For much of my career, my pizza of choice was Lean Cuisine's Deep Dish Three Meat Pizza. I had a freezer full of them. Then one day, the unthinkable happened: Lean

Cuisine discontinued my pizza. This rocked my world. I thought our relationship was forever. I scoured the city buying the remaining stock, but that was a short-term fix. Something was going to have to change. I spent some time on the rebound, seeing other pizzas and having a series of one-lunch stands. I was hesitant to enter into another long-term pizza relationship because the pain was too fresh. But with time comes healing, and I'm happy to share that I've entered into a committed relationship with Red Baron's Meat Trio Deep Dish Singles.

People (including my family) would ask me how I can stand to eat the same thing **every day**? Besides it just being weird, wasn't I bored of those things? For me, not only were they comfortably familiar but it was one less decision I had to make every day. My days at work were full of decisions that had to be made. It was a relief for me to not have to put any thought into what I was going to have for breakfast and lunch.

I share all of this not to provide evidence of what an odd person I am, but to demonstrate the degree to which I take comfort in the familiar. When I say that I prefer for things not to change, I mean it at a pretty extreme level.

Wish Versus Reality

Wish

I take comfort in familiarity, so I prefer for things not to change. I want everything and everybody around me to stay just as they are. This includes change "to" me and change to others around me. I've lived in the same house for decades. I've had the same haircut my whole adult life. In high school, the girl I had a crush on changed her hairstyle, and I was devastated because she didn't look like she was "supposed" to. Things get fixed in my head as being the way they're "supposed to be."

If I like something, I never get bored with it. The Beach Boys and The Beatles have been my favorite bands since 3rd grade. It's never changed. I've listened to their albums thousands of times, and it never gets old. And while I enjoy exploring new places, I'm also happy to keep vacationing at the same spots and repeating things that I enjoy. I have a high capacity for repetition.

Reality

But we all know that change is constant. In the work context, there will be changes to personnel, to responsibilities, to organization structures, to company policies, to the tools and systems you use to do your job, and to the processes you're asked to follow. It feels like as soon as you get comfortable, **something** is going to change.

Ultimately, people who don't handle change well have a hard time being happy and a hard time being successful. Regardless of my preferences, I had to find a way to get comfortable with and embrace change.

Mitigation

During my career, I found three techniques that assisted me in overcoming my tendency to resist change.

Explore the Change

When a change is being made in the business world, there's always a reason for it. I may not like it and I may not agree with it, but there's a reason. When informed of a change, I found that the best first question to ask is "why." If I can understand the reason the change is being made, it helps me get comfortable with and get behind the change.

My next goal was to start thinking of advantages. In almost every scenario, even if there were aspects of the change that I didn't agree with, I could find something that I could sincerely agree was good for the company or my team.

I spent a large part of my career working in one office building. It was kind of old and run-down, but it was familiar and comfortable. Then one day, we were informed that we were moving to a new office building. My instinctive reaction was "But I don't want to move!"

But instead, I asked "why?" The answer was pretty simple and logical: we had space available at another building, and this would let us consolidate and shut down an entire location so the company could save money. OK, that's reasonable and hard to argue with.

How about advantages? Even if I agreed with the logic of the decision, wasn't it just going to be a disruption for my team and for me? Well, as I thought about it, I realized we were going to be moving into a newer building and our new area would be built from scratch. So instead of decades-old furniture and carpet, we'd have new stuff. I could get excited about that. Also, in our old building, we didn't have space for my team to sit together. We were scattered all around the building. That made it harder for us to have a cohesive team atmosphere. In the new building, we were going to all be sitting next to each other in one area. I could get excited about that too.

Now, instead of just being annoyed and stressed by the change, I could agree that there were valid reasons for it, plus there were aspects of it that I was legitimately enthusiastic about.

Exploring the change, both the reasons behind it and the advantages of it, put me in a position where I personally could embrace the change, which then put me in a position where I could help others on my team understand and embrace the change.

Know Thyself

I'm a processor. I need time to process and organize things in my head before knowing how I feel about them. I know that "in the moment," I'm usually **always** going to react negatively to a change. So, I learned to work on my "poker face" when told of changes. I would try to stay neutral and not let myself react. Instead, I would ask clarifying questions to make sure I understood the details of the change and the reasons for the change. But I wouldn't give an opinion on the change. I would sleep on it before discussing it further. I was then prepared the next day to come back and ask any questions I had about the change, including about any remaining concerns, and do it in a calm, nonreactive manner.

This self-awareness helped me avoid coming across as a negative person who was resistant to change, which is not a reputation anyone wants to have.

Understand That Practice Makes "Better"

Experience with change increases confidence. The more change you successfully navigate, the more comfortable you get that you'll be able to do the same with subsequent changes.

My career is a good example of that. During my 30+ years in the corporate world, I changed jobs nine times. The vast majority of those involved taking new jobs within the same company, but a job change is a big deal regardless of whether you're changing companies or not. On average, I was changing jobs every 3-4 years. But there was one period where I felt like I was changing jobs constantly. In a 6-year span, I changed jobs five times within my company.

Someone might look at that and conclude that I was someone who sought out change. That was definitely not the case. In fact, the majority of those changes were not ones I sought out or applied for. Instead, in most cases, I was happily focusing on my current job when I was tapped on the shoulder by company management and asked to take on a different role, because there was a problem they thought I could help with and/or they were trying to develop me.

Along the way, I became more and more comfortable and confident in making those changes.

The first time I changed jobs, I spent days agonizing over it. I made pros and cons lists. I talked with multiple people to get their advice. I changed my mind every 5 minutes. I turned the job down, mostly because of my fear of change. And then I immediately regretted it. Fortunately, they called me back a few weeks later and asked if they could do anything to change my mind. I said, "Yes, offer me the job again." And thank God too, because that job is where I met my wife and that was the job that really launched my career.

The next time I had a job change opportunity, I still spent days agonizing over it and developing a pros/cons list. But at least I actually accepted it this time instead of saying "no" out of a fear of change.

I had a couple of other job changes, each one with some protracted analysis, but I found it was getting easier and less stressful. Then came the day when I was tapped on the shoulder with an opportunity and told I didn't have time to sleep on it. They needed a decision that day.

Had it been a few years prior, I would have said "no" out of fear. But my experience and success with change had given me the confidence I needed to give an immediate answer. I had changed jobs a number of times, and things had always worked out. I said "yes."

As subsequent job opportunities came up during my career, I really barely thought about it. If it was something I was being asked to do by company leadership and/or something I was excited about, I'd just say "yes" and skip doing the analysis. I knew I'd be OK.

And I learned the benefits that came with being open to change. Yes, avoiding change might have been more comfortable. But by embracing change, I got to learn new things, develop new skills, and work with different people. It enriched my life in many ways. If I had let myself give in to my fear of change, I would have missed out on a lot.

Turning It Into a Strength

As I focused on mitigating my resistance to change, I found that I had counter-intuitively become good at being able to lead and help others through changes.

Because I struggle with change, I have to intentionally explore and understand changes to get comfortable. I work to understand the reasons behind the change and try to identify advantages. I spend time processing the change and sorting through any concerns I might have.

As a result of these efforts, I'm in position to help others through their change curve and ultimately be a champion of the change. There were times in my career when my manager communicated a change like an automaton. It was obvious that the decision was coming from "above" and they were just reading the talking points they were given. They didn't really seem to "own" the message and just didn't seem very "real" about it. It could be a very *Stepford Wives* type of experience: "This is what's happening. It's great and we're all happy about it." (Cue creepy smile)

That wasn't me. Because of the amount of energy I put into exploring changes, I was able to be a lot more "real" about it and personalize the conversation. "This is what's happening. These are the reasons for it. Here are the concerns I had when I first heard about it and how I've resolved those concerns in my mind. Here are some things that I think might be challenges and my thoughts on how to approach them. And here are the things that I'm excited about." I always made sure I was supportive of the change, but I was willing to acknowledge concerns and challenges (always with the message that we'd sort through them and adjust as needed).

Taking this approach not only comes across as a lot more genuine than the robotic regurgitation of canned talking points, but it helps others go through their own personal change curve more quickly. I also found that by being more "real," I was able to be a more effective champion of the change than the person who takes the "rah-rah, everything is perfect" approach. I (hopefully) was able to build up trust and credibility by being balanced in communications.

Summary and Next Steps

Some of us take comfort in the familiar. But change is going to happen whether we like it or not. We have to learn how to handle it in a healthy way if we're going to be successful at work (and in our lives).

It's important to be conscious of your tendencies to resist change and to develop techniques to help you handle change constructively. This chapter described examples of those techniques:

- Explore the change: Spend time understanding the reasons behind it and the potential advantages of it.
- Know thyself: If you're a "processor," don't let yourself react to change in the moment. Ask clarifying questions to make sure you understand the details of and the reasons for the change, but sleep on it before expressing an opinion.
- Understand that practice makes "better": The more change you successfully navigate, the more comfortable you'll become in your ability to do the same with subsequent changes. Use that understanding as a catalyst to say "yes" to potential changes in your job and career and start building up your change-navigation experience.

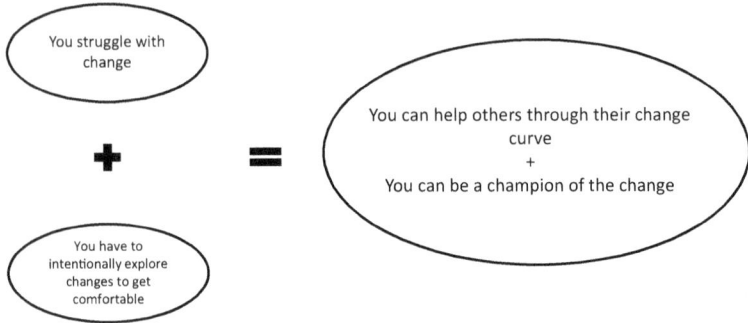

Figure 4.1 Example of how resistance to change can be turned into a strength

Ultimately, it's a mindset shift. With focus, instead of being a change opponent, you can be a champion of change and in position to assist others as they move through their own personal change curves (see Figure 4.1).

CHAPTER 5

Observation 5: Everyone (Else) Is Awesome

(aka How to Overcome Imposter Syndrome and an Inferiority Complex)

There's a theory, popularized by Malcolm Gladwell, that the key to becoming an expert in something is to do it for 10,000 hours.[1]

I have over 30 years of experience, all of it in one field. If I assume that I worked 48 weeks per year and 40 hours per week (which is certainly an underestimation), then I spent 4-to-5 times the amount of time "required" to become an expert in both the audit/security field and in being a leader of IT organizations.

So, I'm good to go, right? I'm a confident expert who knows he can get the job done. Right? (Awkward silence…) Right? (More silence, getting more awkward…)

Wish Versus Reality

Wish

Gladwell would probably say that I'm misusing his theory, but the point is I did my job for a long time. I had plenty of successes during that time. I have every reason to be confident in my abilities.

I want to walk into any meeting or situation with confidence that I'll be able to contribute. Confidence that I'll be able to answer questions that might come my way. Confidence that I'll be able to do the work. Confidence that I won't embarrass myself in front of everyone.

And I want to be able to take it in stride when I make mistakes. I want to process them in the context of all of the successes I've had. I mean, we all make mistakes, right? We're only human. Just learn from it and move on. I certainly give that advice to others. I want to be able to act on the same advice for myself.

Reality

Instead, I have an inferiority complex. I tend to assume that everyone (except me) is capable and confident. I'm frequently asking, "Why can't I be like that person?" I'm basically impressed with everyone but myself. This can lead to me being overly deferential to others (because I think they're so capable and I'm not) and to three other specific issues:

Fear of Making Mistakes

All I remember are my mistakes. Every mistake I've ever made is burned into my brain. I actually think my brain hates me. It's compiled a "greatest hits" playlist of my mistakes, all the way back to childhood, and plays them on "shuffle" throughout the day. I'll be sitting around minding my own business, maybe reading a book or trying to enjoy a show, and out of nowhere the memory of something dumb I did in the past will pop into my head. It could be something from 6th grade, and I'll still feel the same negative emotions I felt when it happened. It's like it happened yesterday. That embarrassing thing I did on a date back in 1990? I'm suddenly feeling that same embarrassment and asking myself how I could be so stupid, wondering "what is wrong with me?" The time I spend in the shower is the worst, because there's nothing to distract me from the barrage of bad memories. I shared that with a friend once and received a waterproof Bluetooth speaker as a gift. I now listen to music in the shower. It's a nice distraction. And better than the alternative I considered of giving up bathing.

I'm pretty much bombarded by these memories every day. The memories of all of the successes? Things that would make me feel good about myself? Those don't pop into my head for some reason. Just the bad stuff.

In addition to being unpleasant, there's a practical impact from all of this revisiting of my mistakes. It can lead to a fear of making another mistake (because I don't want another one added to the playlist) and devastation when I do make one ("there's another one that I'll be replaying forever"). If I'm not careful, it can lead to me being overly cautious about taking risks, and it can cause me to be too slow to bounce back when the inevitable mistake happens. My tendency is to beat myself up and over-apologize when I make a mistake. I'm quick to give others grace for making a mistake but struggle to give that same grace to myself.

Imposter Syndrome

I continue to experience imposter syndrome. If you're not familiar with the term, imposter syndrome is what it sounds like—the feeling that you're an imposter, along with the ever-present fear that you'll be discovered as being a fraud. One of the clearest definitions I've found says that imposter syndrome is "the condition of feeling anxious and not experiencing success internally, despite being high-performing in external, objective ways. This condition often results in people feeling like 'a fraud' or 'a phony' and doubting their abilities."[2] *Psychology Today* says, "People who struggle with imposter syndrome believe that they are undeserving of their achievements and the high esteem in which they are, in fact, generally held. They feel that they aren't as competent or intelligent as others might think—and that soon enough, people will discover the truth about them."[3]

Following the example of Paul the Apostle,[*] I'll do something that's uncomfortable and out of character for me: I'll boast. I have over 30 years of experience. I was promoted through "the ranks" at my company, first through successes as a technical individual contributor and then through various management positions, eventually becoming a senior executive. I wrote a book about my area of expertise that was published by a major publishing house and did well enough to warrant a second and then a third edition. I've spoken at major conferences and taught college courses in my field.

---

[*]I'm referring to (and wildly misusing) 2 Corinthians 11-12.

If I were to read that resume for someone else, it would leave me with a positive impression about that person. I would assume they were an expert and have confidence that they knew what they were doing. Yet, I've never been able to reach the same conclusion about myself. I experienced imposter syndrome every day throughout my career.

In fact, as silly as it sounds, when I finally retired from my company, my internal feeling was, "Wow, I really dodged a bullet. I somehow managed to make it through more than 30 years on the job without people realizing that I don't know what I'm doing. Phew." After I decided to retire, but before it was announced, instead of being able to finally relax, I spent the next weeks in fear that I'd be "found out" and discovered as an imposter when I was so close to the finish line. Objectively, I knew it was ridiculous, but it didn't make it any less real to me.

By all objective standards, I had a successful career. Yet, I experienced imposter syndrome until the end. If you do too, you're in good company. Don't let it hold you back. Understand that it's your brain misbehaving, basically trying to trick you into believing something that's not true, and learn how to mitigate it.

Unhealthy Response to Feedback

Part of working in any workplace is receiving feedback, both in the form of formal performance reviews and in the form of ad hoc feedback throughout the year. Feedback is good for us and is part of how we grow.

But because of my challenges with imposter syndrome and fear of making mistakes, I can have an unhealthy response when given feedback. My most common tendency is to go into a spiral of self-negativity, beating myself up, and losing what little self-confidence I have. But there are also occasions where the opposite will happen. I'll be tired of beating myself up and want to allow myself to display confidence. That's all well and good, but at times I'll overcorrect and become defensive, arguing with the feedback.

Neither of these are healthy responses to receiving feedback.

Mitigation

You want to find a way to derail your career? How about undervaluing yourself, being in a constant negativity spiral, refusing to take any risks due to fear of failure, and being overly deferential to all of your co-workers? Yeah, that will do it. I had to figure out a way out of that pattern. There were a few things that helped.

Be Nice to Yourself

Anyone who watched *Saturday Night Live* in the early 90s is probably familiar with Stuart Smalley, a character created and performed by Al Franken. In the skits with Smalley, he hosts a self-help show called *Daily Affirmation with Stuart Smalley*, where he encourages his viewers to avoid stinkin' thinkin' and practice positive self-talk: "I'm entitled to my share of happiness." "I refuse to beat myself up." "I'm good enough, I'm smart enough, and doggone it, people like me." If you want to be truly inspired, find the video on YouTube of Michael Jordan on Stuart's show saying that last one.[4]

While these skits were played for laughs, as I've gotten older, I've realized that there's actually something to them. My default is to fill my head with negative thoughts. In addition to that "greatest hits" playlist of my mistakes that runs through my head, I think the most frequent words out of my mouth are "I'm so stupid," "I'm such an idiot," "What is wrong with me?" and of course the classic "I hate myself." The deep cut "I'm worthless" makes an appearance in the rotation at times too. These comments to myself don't exactly put me in a position to overcome my inferiority complex and enter a situation with confidence. Instead, they accentuate those negative feelings.

While I don't go so far as to stare in a mirror and say nice things to myself, like Smalley did, I have found that cutting off the flow of negative comments and thoughts and replacing them with something positive places me in a much better headspace.

So, how do you stop that flow of negative memories and comments? That's hard for me, because the first step is actually **wanting** to stop them. I usually feel that I deserve those negative thoughts and comments, so why should I stop them? It's what I have coming to me.

But I once had a friend ask me, "Would you ever talk to someone else like that?" The answer was a strong, "No! I would never speak to another human being like that!" Could you imagine telling someone that you hate them or that they're stupid or that they're worthless? OK, OK, I guess there are times I've **imagined** saying things like that when someone has done something truly egregious to me that impacted me on a profound and personal level, such as a batter on my favorite baseball team hitting into a double play with the bases loaded to end an inning. But I would never in a million years actually *say* those words to someone.

My friend then asked me if I would tolerate it if I heard someone speaking to another person like that. The answer again was, no, I would be deeply disturbed by it and I hope I would step in to stop the verbal abuse. I'm even bothered when athletes are booed on the field. I might withhold my applause, but I'll never boo a person. It just doesn't seem very nice.

So, then he asked me, "Why do you think it's OK to talk to yourself like that?" I found that to be a profound question. The book of Genesis states that we're all created in God's image.[†] *The Declaration of Independence* of the United States says that "all men are created equal."[‡] The great Ray Davies tells us that we are all God's children.[§5] Bottom line, you can find plenty of backing, both religious and secular, for the concept that every person has intrinsic value and that it's not OK to abuse anyone. It's something I firmly believe. Sometimes I might not **feel** like I have a lot of value, but I can't escape the logic:

- All human beings have intrinsic value and deserve to be treated with respect
- I'm a human being

[†]Genesis 1:27.

[‡]From *The Declaration of Independence*, which can be found online at www.archives.gov/founding-docs/declaration.

[§]Ray Davies was the leader of the rock band The Kinks (one of the greatest bands of all time by the way).

- Therefore, I have intrinsic value and deserve to be treated with respect.

Once I figured that out, it made it much easier to actually **want** to stop all of those negative memories and self-comments.

The next step was actually doing it. Easier said than done. For me, it was mostly about focus. When one of those memories of a mistake starts playing in my head, instead of letting the memory play out (along with all of the negative feelings and self-flagellation that go along with it), I can make the decision to think about something, anything, else. I can think about a recent or upcoming vacation. I can say a prayer. I can make a mental list of every past World Series winner. I can think about who I hope wins this season of *The Great British Baking Show*. There are so many options. The point is to redirect my brain and change the channel on that negative memory. It's even better if I can change the channel from a negative memory to a positive one, something that might build me up instead of tearing me down, but I don't always have time to browse the channel guide and find the best alternate program. I just need to change the TV from the current channel as quickly as possible and grab the first thought that will distract me.

And when I start making those negative "I'm so stupid" sorts of comments to myself, I can just stop the flow of words. Just make the decision to not say those things to myself. I had a therapist who recommended that I go the Stuart Smalley route and say positive things to myself instead. She recommended that I verbalize statements and refer to myself in the third person, such as "Mike is smart and is going to do a great job on his presentation." I tried it for about a minute but just couldn't do it. It might be a great technique for others, but I couldn't get past how silly I felt. For one thing, it went against my personal policy of never, ever referring to myself in the third person (Mike just doesn't do that). But I could certainly stop the flow of negative comments toward myself. And I can instead try to focus on affirming feedback I've received from others. I have a few go-to comments I've received from family, friends, and co-workers that I can call up on demand to remind myself that maybe I'm not so bad, even after I feel I've done something wrong.

I actually have a physical mechanism for redirecting all of these negative thoughts. When I realize my brain is taking me down a negative path, I'll make a fist and tap on my leg or my head as sort of a physical prompt to change the channel in my head. I prefer to knock on my head because that's where the thoughts are coming from, but that might look a little weird if I'm sitting in a meeting. But I can rap my knuckles on my leg without it being too noticeable.

Caveat

Self-refection and humility are important. It's critical that we all analyze our actions. It's how we identify opportunities for improvement. It's how we self-correct. It's how we realize that we might need to make amends with someone. The advice to redirect negative thoughts is not intended to prevent valuable self-reflection. It's to avoid going down a path of spiraling negativity and psychological self-harm. Self-reflection is good. Self-flagellation isn't. It's the difference between having a healthy humility versus having an inferiority complex.

While these methods weren't a magic pill for removing my imposter syndrome or inferiority complex, they helped. By not constantly bombarding myself with negativity about myself, and replacing it with something positive, I found that it was much better. Not perfect, but manageable.

Have the Right Mindset When Receiving Feedback

We all should be on the path of continuous improvement. That's something I firmly believe in life and certainly is the case at work. One of the most valuable mechanisms for being able to improve is receiving feedback from others. We can often be too close to our own performance and behaviors to objectively evaluate them. We need input from others, whether our boss or our co-workers or our friends or our family.

But if we want to receive feedback from people, we need to make it as pleasant as possible for people to give us feedback. How we receive feedback has a direct impact on people's interest and willingness in giving it to us. We, therefore, all have a responsibility to make it easy for people to give us feedback.

If a co-worker gives me feedback, and I respond by becoming offended and arguing with them, will they ever want to give me feedback again? Probably not, which means I'll be losing valuable input that could help me with my goal of continuous improvement.

I mentioned earlier that my default response to feedback was beating myself up and spiraling into negativity. Let's see what that might look like.

Boss: Hi Mike, do you have a minute? I have some feedback on that email you sent to the CEO yesterday.

Me: Oh no. What did I do? How bad is it?

Boss: No, no, it's fine. You got your message across, but there were a few spots where I thought you could have been clearer and where I thought you could have used less words. No big deal – just some things that I thought might be helpful for next time.

Me: I knew I should have let you review it before I sent it. I'm so sorry. I'll do better next time.

Boss: No apology needed. It's really not a big deal. I just wanted to share my thoughts. (Proceeds to share minor comments on the email)

Me: I can't believe I sent an email to the CEO with those stupid mistakes. How dumb can I be? Do I need to send him a follow-up?

Boss: No, like I said, it's fine. It's just some minor feedback. I'm sure he didn't even notice anything.

Me: Well, I'm really, really sorry about this. I expect better of myself and I know you expect better of me. I just can't believe I was so stupid. I wouldn't blame you if you never trusted me to send another message to the CEO again.

Boss: (Proceeds to spend the next 5 minutes reassuring me that I'm OK and consoling me, all the while thinking about how what she envisioned as a 2 minute conversation somehow turned into a 15 minute conversation. And wondering why she even bothered to share the feedback with me.)

Think about that from the standpoint of the feedback giver. It's exhausting. All my boss wanted to do was share some minor feedback in the interest of my ongoing development and improvement. It took way longer than it needed to, and it turned into a counseling session, where she had to spend time and energy reassuring me that I'm not an awful person. The next time something similar happens, where there's an opportunity for minor coaching, is she going to bother coming by and sharing her thoughts with me? Or is she going to think about how much time it's going to take to not only give me the feedback but then "talk me down" from my self-recriminations, ultimately deciding that maybe the feedback isn't so important after all and she'll just skip talking with me? If the latter, I've just missed out on an opportunity to receive valuable input that might help me in the future, all because of my poor skills in receiving feedback.

As a long-time manager, I gave feedback to people countless times. My least favorite type of person to give feedback to was The Arguer. The Arguer was the person who would argue every point I made. For each specific example I provided, they would have some extenuating circumstance as a reason for why their poor performance in that instance should be excused. They would at times go on the attack, explaining how their poor performance was really someone else's fault, maybe even mine (e.g., I didn't communicate clearly, I didn't support them). Or they would bring up unrelated grievances to deflect the conversation. The one thing they wouldn't do? Take ownership of the issue and commit to improving. I would leave those conversations exhausted and annoyed. I would also leave hoping to never have to have another feedback session with that person. Of course, as their boss, it was my job to give them feedback, so I couldn't avoid it. But the bar for what feedback was worth giving might become higher. It became a cost/benefit analysis each time: "Is this feedback important enough to be worth the pain? Or is it something I can live with?" If the latter, I might just keep it to myself. The result? That person cost themselves an opportunity to receive valuable input that might help them in the future. (And that's not to even mention the fact that those "arguing" behaviors are a negative that will impact a person's performance evaluation and ultimately their compensation.)

Because I wanted to continuously improve and I knew that receiving feedback was critical if I wanted to do so, my goal was to make it easy for people to give me feedback. I did so by following a simple process:

1. **Always start by thanking people for giving you feedback.** They're doing you a favor, so express appreciation.

2. **Never argue the feedback in the moment.** Ask clarification questions to make sure you understand it, but don't argue it. You might not agree with it, but the feedback is what the feedback is. It's what the other person perceives, and you need to understand that perception. Arguing the feedback gets in the way of that.

3. **Separate the message from how the message is delivered.** Sometimes a person might deliver feedback in a rude and offensive way. But if you focus solely on being offended by how the message was delivered, you might fail to hear an important message that you can use to improve yourself.

   I was in a meeting once where a peer called me "clueless" in a room full of people. I was seething. I mean, that's just inexcusably rude, plus embarrassing. All I could think about was how offended I was and how much I really didn't like that person anymore. I certainly didn't care about why that person thought I was clueless. But once I calmed down, I realized that I needed to understand the comment. So, I had a conversation with her and asked. I found out that my tendency to stay calm during a crisis came across to her as me not understanding how important the situation was. She thought I was being lackadaisical and just not getting that there was an important problem to be resolved. It was valuable feedback and let me tweak my behavior. I still stayed calm during a crisis, but I started verbalizing my understanding of how critical the situation was so that people would know that I "got it" and that I was going to act with a sense of urgency.

Separately, I also had a conversation with her about how I didn't appreciate her making that comment in front of everyone. She apologized and the whole situation strengthened our relationship.

If I had just focused on being offended by the jerky way the message was delivered, I would have missed out on valuable feedback. The message was legitimate and valuable. It was just delivered poorly.

4. **Focus on what to do differently versus beating yourself up**. What's done is done. You can't change the past but you can learn from it and avoid making the same mistake in the future. When I receive feedback, I always assume there's something in the feedback I can use to improve. While my instinct is to beat myself up and add it to my playlist of mistakes, I instead refocus my brain to develop a plan for what I'm going to do differently in response to that feedback.

5. **Follow up with the feedback giver**. Once you've had the chance to process the feedback, follow back up with the person who gave you the feedback. Use it as an opportunity to thank them again. Tell them what you've decided to do to address the feedback. If you need additional clarification on the feedback, ask for it. If you have a different perspective that you think is important to share, now is the time to do it. Doing so when you're receiving the feedback comes across as arguing. Calmly sharing your perspective after taking time to process the feedback is much more likely to come across as thoughtful and collaborative, but it still should be done in a way that is not dismissive of the feedback.

Following back up with the feedback giver is a powerful way to show appreciation for the feedback and also that you're taking it seriously. This makes it much more likely that you'll continue receiving valuable feedback in the future.

Learn How to Accept Compliments

I'm uncomfortable with compliments. If someone compliments me for something, I want to explain to the person that, yes, I might have done this one thing well but I'm aware of all of my many flaws and I don't deserve any praise. Somehow, I feel that if I accept the compliment, then that means that I think that I'm deserving of the compliment and that will come across as arrogant. How twisted is that logic? "Yeah, I got lucky and did this one thing well, but I want to make sure you know that I know that I really suck."

Years ago, I took over a job from someone who had been struggling in the role. After a few months, a co-worker came into my office to praise me, telling me how much better things were and what a great job I was doing. My thought was that, since my predecessor struggled, the bar was pretty low for me to look good. So, I responded to her very thoughtful and sincere compliments by dismissively saying something like, "Well, thanks but they could have put a mannequin in this chair and things would have gotten better." I thought this comment was just me showing appropriate humility. But the look on my co-worker's face made me pause. She reacted to my comment like it was slap in the face. She seemed dejected.

This exchange caused me to rethink my approach to receiving compliments. What I realized was that what I had done wasn't laudable humility; it was me being disrespectful to the person complimenting me and disregarding her opinion. She had come into my office to very kindly share a thoughtful compliment with me, and I just slapped it away.

A simple "thank you" works nicely. Keep it simple. When someone gives you a compliment, tell them how much you appreciate it and then shut up.

Turning It Into a Strength

How does one turn an inferiority complex into a strength?

Well, I had the following two aspects of my personality as "inputs" into this equation:

- I'm hyper aware of my shortcomings.
- I have innate respect for others' abilities.

Once I had mitigated some of the "derailer" aspects of my inferiority complex, as discussed earlier in this chapter, and had gotten it under some sort of control, I found that it actually did give me some advantages:

- I stay grounded and avoid over-confidence.
- I take others' ideas and inputs seriously.

Staying Grounded and Avoiding Over-Confidence

Imposter syndrome gives you a natural humility. I never had a "Fat Elvis" period. I never felt like I had "made it" and could stop learning and growing. I was driven throughout my career to improve my skills and my value.

Taking Others' Ideas and Inputs Seriously

We covered earlier in this chapter the importance of receiving feedback from others in an open-minded way so that we can stay on the path of continuous improvement. That's certainly one aspect of taking others' ideas and inputs seriously, but it goes beyond that.

I've been in meetings where it was clear that the senior leader at the table thought that he was the smartest person in the room. All ideas flowed from him. Dissenting ideas were quickly argued away and sometimes even mocked. People quickly learned that there was no point in speaking their minds and providing their ideas. The result? The organization was limited to the ideas of just one person. I've seen similar scenarios where it wasn't a senior leader creating this scenario but just the "loudest voice in the room": a person who was sure he was right and shouted down everyone else, to the point where the rest of the room shut down.

This approach is not the way to maximize your chances for success, as an individual or as an organization.

I never thought I was the smartest person in the room (far from it). Now, I had to stop feeling like I was the dumbest person in the room, as described earlier in the chapter. But once I had done that, the natural humility that came with my inferiority complex meant that I was always open to others' ideas. I might have been the senior person in the room, but I didn't think all ideas had to come from me (and in fact, didn't want all ideas to come from me). In those instances where I was that senior person in the room, I would generally try to give my ideas and opinions last, so that I didn't unintentionally discourage the flow of thought.

To put it in *Star Trek* terms (in other words, in the best terms possible), I followed the Captain Picard, not the Captain Kirk, style of leadership and decision making. Kirk frequently made snap decisions, without seeking input from others. Picard would usually gather his senior officers around a conference room table to gather options and opinions before making a decision.

Kirk's style made for a more action-packed episode, but I think the Picard style is generally better in real life. Seeking ideas and opinions from others (and taking them seriously) leads not only to more informed decisions but also to increased buy-in from the team that will be implementing those decisions. I have found that people are generally much quicker to get on board with a decision if they've had the opportunity to provide input and they feel like their input was "heard," even if ultimately the decision went a different way than they had recommended.

Obviously, as with all things, discernment is important. Not all topics are appropriate for discussion with others (such as discussions involving personnel matters or other sensitive information). Sometimes speed is of the essence, and you just can't take the time to gather inputs. And you won't always be able to reach consensus. You have to know when you've reached the point of "analysis paralysis" and just make a decision.

Summary and Next Steps

Having an inferiority complex is no fun, and it can lead to issues in the workplace, such as:

- Fear of making mistakes
- Imposter syndrome
- Unhealthy response to feedback

Finding ways to address and overcome these self-esteem issues is critical not only for your career but also for your mental health and personal happiness. It won't happen without intentionally identifying and implementing techniques to help you do so, such as the examples covered in this chapter:

- Be nice to yourself: First and foremost, understand that it's not OK to beat yourself up and that you need to treat yourself with the same respect as you would treat anyone else. Cut off and redirect the negative thoughts, memories, and self-comments, replacing them with something positive.
- Have the right mindset when receiving feedback: Understand that we all need feedback if we want to be successful, so it's important to make it easy for others to give it to you. Thank people for giving you feedback. Ask clarifying questions about the feedback but don't argue it in the moment. Separate the

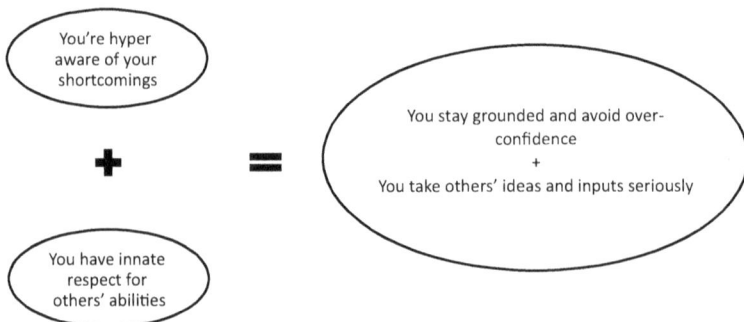

Figure 5.1 Example of how imposter syndrome and an inferiority complex can be turned into a strength

message from how it's delivered. Focus on what to do differently instead of beating yourself up. And circle back with the feedback giver regarding how you plan to address their inputs.

- Learn how to accept compliments: Learn to get comfortable with compliments instead of arguing with or dismissing them. A simple "thank you" suffices.

With focus, that low self-confidence can be turned into a healthy humility that brings with it some advantages, including staying grounded and taking others' ideas and inputs seriously (see Figure 5.1).

CHAPTER 6

Observation 6: Relaxation? What's That?

(aka How to Give Your Brain a Break From Constantly Worrying About Work)

You've got to be kidding me.

I was finally able to relax. I was retired from my high-stress job and after a few decades of never being able to settle my brain down, the most stressful thing I had to worry about was whether I could catch up on watching the shows on my DVR before it became full and started deleting things.

Then, I started writing this book. I intentionally decided to write most of it before having any sort of contract with a publisher so that I wouldn't have any deadlines or pressure. I wanted to do it at my own pace. I started out fine, working on it for a couple of hours each morning and then forgetting about it. But it didn't take long before I found myself thinking about it all of the time, turning over in my head all of the things I still had left to do and how I might improve the manuscript. I'd be trying to read a book or sit and watch a baseball game, and my mind would start picking at things I needed to do. Pretty soon, I'd give up and be back in my office working on it. It became like a full-time job, and I actually started feeling stress over it.

And this was for something that *literally* no one was asking for or waiting on. If I stopped working on it, there would be zero repercussions and not a person on the planet would care.

Seriously?

What the @#&$ is wrong with me?

Wish Versus Reality

Wish

I'm not a "live to work" guy. I always thought of my job as a means to an end. When people would ask me what my career goal was, my glib answer was often "retirement." I want to be able to relax, plus I know work isn't as high of a priority as family and faith. I felt like I had my priorities straight, in my head at least.

Reality

I can't stop thinking about work. My brain is constantly spinning, figuring out how to resolve current problems, dissecting and examining recent actions, crafting communications (such as how to best respond to that request for information or that angry email I received), and planning for upcoming meetings, projects, and presentations. It's exhausting in there. And it's hard to get it to stop.

What's worse, I often think that I **shouldn't** get it to stop. My fear is that the constant worry and overthinking about work is part of my "process" and that if I let up, I'll "lose it" and stop being successful. Maybe that nonstop mental activity is the only thing propping me up and keeping me from being discovered for the fraud I am (going back to the imposter syndrome covered in the previous chapter).

This approach can lead to constant stress and mental fatigue. And that can lead to burnout, which can have a detrimental impact on your career (not to mention your happiness). There are also other, practical repercussions. Because I know that anything I sign up for is going to be added to the list of things that I worry and stress over, it makes me slow to want to volunteer for things. There were often times I'd be in a staff meeting, and my boss would ask for a volunteer for something. It could be as simple as needing an executive sponsor for a team (meaning that other people would be doing all of the work). My peers' hands would shoot up immediately, but I'd be hesitant, not wanting to add something else to my "worry" pile. I might eventually think about it and decide it was the right thing to do, but I was slow on the draw and often someone else had already volunteered while I was busy processing. The problem with that is the optics could be bad, giving me the appearance of not being a team player, since I'm not volunteering to help out as often as others. And that hesitation could lead to me not having some rewarding experiences and opportunities.

A side note to bosses: Consider giving advance notice of things you're going to need volunteers for. Don't ask for a volunteer "in the moment," where the quickest hand to be raised is the winner. Understand that some people are processors and are going to think before volunteering. Those people who volunteer after processing and considering it are likely to be fully committed to the task and do a good job, so level the playing field for different personality types to make sure they're not shut out.

Mitigation

Redirecting your brain from constant worry about work is, as with so many things in life, easier said than done. And, as should be clear from the opening story in this chapter, it's not something I've mastered.

The first thing I had to overcome was my fear that the constant worrying about work was essential to my success. In other words, I had to give myself permission to take mental rests. The key for me was the realization that it wasn't worth the price. If business success was going to require me to think about work nonstop (meaning I wouldn't be fully present with my family and would never feel relaxed), I didn't want it.

Once I got over that hurdle, I did find some techniques that helped me give myself a break from the "work worry."

Release It From Your Brain by Writing It Down

There's power in writing things down. As long as something is only in my brain, I can't let it go. If I let it go, I'm worried I'll forget it. I spend a lot of time turning things over in my head to decide what to do about them. I'll eventually arrive at a conclusion or a planned approach. But I feel like I have to keep revisiting it in an endless loop or I'll lose my hard-fought conclusions.

But I've found if I write it down, I can release it and move on to other things. It's like magic for me. It gives me permission to move it out of active memory and into storage, because I know the information I wrote down will give me the key to open that file back up and re-access the information and conclusions whenever I need them.

When I say "write it down," I don't literally mean with a pen and paper (although that's fine if you're old school like that). I mean to record it, however is appropriate. I've found a few methods that work:

Use the Notes App on Your Phone

In the old days, you might have had to carry a pad of paper and a pen with you everywhere you went so that you'd be ready to record your thoughts. Now, everyone's phone should have some sort of notes app. When I'm ready to release something from my brain that I've been working through, I'll often record my thoughts and conclusions in a note on my phone.* Most of us have our phones with us all of the time, even right next to us when we're in bed and we have those middle-of-the-night thought-storms, so this method should always be available when needed.

Draft an Email

Often, the things I'm working on in my head have to do with the best way to communicate or respond to something via email. Maybe I have thoughts on how to respond but I'm not ready to send it yet. It could be after-hours or the weekend, and I don't want to be "that guy" who's sending stuff during nonwork hours (and I also might not want to risk getting a reply before the next work day, which would just start the cycle all over again). Or maybe I want to think on it some more before hitting the "send" button. But if I go ahead and write the email, I can save it as a draft, get it out of my head, and come back to it when I'm ready to send it. And again, with email apps on our phones, this is something

---

*I've also known people who would send themselves an email instead of creating a note.

that I can usually do right away instead of waiting until I'm back in front of a computer.

Create a To-Do List

Sometimes you have to stick with the classics. Nothing beats a good to-do list. If I think of something I need to do, sometimes I'll keep thinking about it and thinking about it because I'm worried that I'll forget to do it. But if I write it on a to-do list, I can stop thinking about it because I know I won't forget. I've done to-do lists on my phone, on paper, and on the whiteboard in my office. It doesn't matter. Just record it somewhere.

Put It on Your Calendar

An alternative to writing it on a to-do list is to schedule it. The problem with to-do lists is that they can get long and you could find yourself worrying that that important thing will get lost on it.

Early in my career, I kept a calendar spreadsheet with to-dos. I would create a spreadsheet with one column for each week of the year. As I got action items, I would go slot them into 1 week of the year, depending on due date and priority. When that week came, I made sure I knocked out all of the to-dos on the calendar for that week, or if something really couldn't get done, moved it to the next week. It was a simple way to make sure nothing was dropped.

Later, I dropped the spreadsheet and started putting to-dos on my online calendar. I need to create a presentation that will be delivered next Thursday? I'll go block an hour for presentation prep time this Tuesday. I need to create that report for the boss? I'll block 30 minutes tomorrow afternoon to get it done. Those dry runs I mentioned in the chapter on public speaking? I'll put them on my calendar in the days leading up to the presentation. Anything to prevent a fire drill and keep me organized.

Once those tasks were on my calendar, I could release them from my brain because I knew I wouldn't forget about them.

Use Your PTO

On a typical weekend, it's usually sometime around Sunday evening before I've finally relaxed and gotten out of "work mode" in my brain. And of course, that's just in time to go back to work the next day. A 2-day weekend just isn't enough time to decompress and get my mind out of its "thinking about work" gear long enough to feel mentally refreshed.

It was only on vacations (whether traveling somewhere or just taking time off at home) that my mental batteries could really recharge and that I felt myself get out of work mode. By the end of a weeklong vacation, I'd find that I really had stopped thinking about work. And that was crucial for my mental health and my ability to avoid burnout on the job, meaning it was good not only for me but for my company.

Whether your company calls it PTO (Paid Time Off), time bank, or vacation days, the point is: use it. By the end of my career, I earned a healthy amount of PTO. And I used every day of it. I almost never carried a balance forward from year to year. At the beginning of each year, I would plan out all of my time off for the year. It helped keep me sane. Knowing that I basically never relax during a normal workweek, I needed to have those mental breaks to look forward to.

I was fortunate to work for a company that respected the need for people to take time off. I had a boss who once used me as an example at a department meeting. He was encouraging people to use their vacation time, because of how important it is for all of us to take breaks. He then pointed to me and said that I always use all of my vacation time and that's what he wanted everyone to do. I felt like a kid whose mom had just praised him for eating all of the food on his plate at dinner.

I've heard horror stories about people working at companies where they're pressured to not take time off. I honestly think I would have had to change companies. And a new trend is companies telling employees that they don't track PTO and that they encourage employees to take time off whenever they need it. They couch it as a good thing: "Hey, just take off whatever time you need." While that sounds good in theory, if you're someone like me who needs frequent time off to avoid burnout, that's just stressful. I would feel enormous pressure to not take time off because I wouldn't want to look like I wasn't working as hard as other people. I need an "entitlement" of time off and a company that supports me in using it.

The key, for me at least, was to work for a company that had a PTO philosophy that met my needs and then to take that time off. That put me in a position to avoid burnout and be more mentally healthy and engaged when at work.

Set Boundaries

In Chapter 7, we're going to discuss the concept of setting boundaries and striking a balance as an important technique for managing stress and anxiety. This concept is especially relevant to redirecting your brain from constant "work worry," so we'll touch on it here as well with some specific examples geared toward the topic of this chapter.

Example 1: Avoid "Checking in" While on Vacation

We discussed the importance of taking PTO in the previous section. For vacations to give me the mental break I need, it's important for me to unplug from work during that time. I had co-workers who were constantly checking and responding to emails while on vacation. That would have totally defeated the purpose of taking the time off for me. Checking emails was stressful enough and would get my head spinning about how to respond or how to deal with the issue or question being presented. It would immediately put me back into "work mode" mentally. But responding to emails? Disaster. As soon as you start responding, the conversation in the office is "Oh yeah, he's on vacation but he's responding to emails, so go ahead and send that to him." You'll start receiving responses to your responses plus additional work and questions, all with an expectation that you'll be taking care of it while you're on your vacation.

I had to establish the boundary that, when I was on vacation, I wasn't checking in with work. On my last day before the break, I would set up an "out of office" auto-reply for my email, stating that I was out of the office and when I would be back, explaining that I wouldn't be replying until my return, and giving an alternate person to contact if they needed an answer in the meantime. That way, expectations would be set for anyone who emailed me. I would tell my closest co-workers that I was going to be out, with instructions to text me if they needed me for something urgent. Taking that approach freed my brain from feeling the need to "check in" with work. I wasn't worried that someone was waiting for me to respond to something urgent, because my "out of office" auto-reply set expectations.

That approach might not work for everyone. I had a peer who told me that my approach would stress him out, because he'd be too anxious about the "unknown" of not knowing what was waiting for him in his inbox. So, his rule while on vacation was to check his email one time per day, and **only** one time per day, usually in the evening when his family had already settled in for the night. That allowed him to put his mind at ease while setting the boundary that he wasn't going to constantly check in throughout the day while on vacation.

Example 2: Protect Your Weekends

I mentioned earlier that I basically didn't get out of mental "work mode" until the weekend was almost over. But even so, that 2 day break was crucial for me to get at least a bit of a mental reset. So, I did everything I could to protect those weekends. We all have times where we need to put in extra hours to meet deadlines. I decided I was going to put **all** of those hours in Monday through Friday so that I could get a break when the weekend came. I would rather work five 16 hour days, knowing I would get a break come the weekend, than spread it out over seven days and never get a break.

Example 3: Take a Break From Your Phone After Hours

Checking email on my phone in the evening just exacerbated my problem of never being able to stop thinking about work. It's so tempting. Maybe it's during a commercial break of a game I'm watching. I don't want to watch the ads, so I grab my phone. I see that I have five new emails. Why not open the email app and clear them out?

The problem with that is that it's like walking through a mine field. I might get lucky and come out unscathed, for example if all five of those emails are innocuous and require nothing much from me. But one of those emails might blow up my evening. Maybe it's my boss giving me an action item. Maybe it's a stakeholder who's angry about something. Maybe it's my team telling me about a problem. Now my evening is destroyed, because that's all I'm going to be able to think about. And it was self-inflicted.

Get a Hobby

Few things are better for taking your mind off of work than getting absorbed in something that you're passionate about. I love to read. And going to baseball games. And listening to music. And listing out my hobbies while writing a book about anxiety. When I'm doing one of those things (well, maybe not that last one), I can find that hours go by and work hasn't even crossed my mind.

There are a million potential hobbies out there (exactly one million; I counted). Hopefully you already have one or more. If not, find one that speaks to you. And carve out time for that hobby. It's an effective way to redirect your brain from thinking about work.

Practice Prayer and Mindfulness

I've found that both prayer and mindfulness are techniques that can help slow my mind down and recenter it, taking it off of all of those work worries. These topics are covered in detail in Chapter 8, which has guidance on creating your own stress-relief toolkit.

Create Routines to Signal to Your Brain That Work Is Over

I'm a creature of habit. I love routines. Kind of like a dog, I guess. I always found the commute home to be valuable, because it signaled to my brain that work was over and I could transition to focusing on other things. I worked with people who liked to be as efficient as possible and would schedule phone meetings to take place while driving home.

I would never do that and absolutely hated it when people called me while I was driving home. I used that time to decompress and shift gears. I would listen to music and try to stop thinking about work, so that I could be in the right mindset when I got home to my family.

And then COVID happened and we stopped going into the office. I never left home. I found it hard to transition out of work mode. I would work all day over VPN from my home office, and it was easy to just let the work day keep going. Maybe I'd leave my home office to have dinner, but then I'd think of something else I needed to do and find myself right back in my office working again. I mean, why wait until tomorrow when I can take care of it now by just walking a few feet back into my home office? Basically, I found myself working all day. I realized that I needed a routine to replace the commute home, something that could give me separation between "work" time and "home" time. I started getting dressed for work at the beginning of the day, putting on something reasonably close to what I'd wear if I were in the office (closer than sweat pants and a T-shirt anyway). At the end of the day, I'd change out of those work clothes. And then I'd take my dog for a walk, listening to music while I did so. I found that those routines were effective in signaling to my brain that work was over, similar to what my commute had done for me previously.

Those are just some examples. The encouragement here is to establish some sort of routine that helps you make that mental shift from "I'm working" to "I'm not working."

Focus on Others

Ultimately all of that worrying about work is a self-centered thing. My mind is spinning, focusing on my own worries and problems. Sometimes the best way to "get over yourself" is to focus on someone else instead. It could be through volunteer work. Or being there for a friend or family member who's going through a hard time. Or mentoring others who are earlier in their careers. There's no shortage of opportunities. When I stop focusing on myself and instead turn my attention to others, those things I was worrying about get put in perspective and become less "ever present" in my mind.

Turning It Into a Strength

I think the "strength" part of this topic is probably pretty obvious. Because of my tendency to constantly think about work, I was an extremely conscientious employee. I was always going to be thoughtful and thorough in how I approached things, thinking things through from all angles. I would consider and prepare for any eventuality.

The potential career derailers here were burnout, plus the situation I described earlier of being slow to volunteer when opportunities arose. By putting guardrails in place to stop my mind from constantly worrying about work, I was able to mitigate both of those things. I gave myself enough mental breaks to avoid burnout. And I was more willing to raise my hand and volunteer, because I knew I'd be able to protect myself from being overwhelmed by the addition of "one more thing" to worry about.

Summary and Next Steps

Those of us with high anxiety can often find it impossible to turn our brains off and stop thinking about work, which can lead to burnout and an inability to enjoy life.

If this describes you, you'll want to develop and commit to techniques to improve your mental work-life balance, such as the ones described in this chapter:

- Release it from your brain by writing it down: Whether it's using the Notes app on your phone, drafting and saving an email to be sent later, creating a to-do list, putting it on your calendar, or a combination of those things, there's power in writing things down so that you can let it go from being front-of-mind.
- Use your PTO: Taking extended time away from work is often the best way to mentally recharge and get out of work mode.

- Set boundaries: Make sure you're setting up guardrails to help you strike a balance in your life and give yourself a break from thinking about work, such as avoiding "checking in" when on vacation, protecting your weekends, and taking a break from your phone after hours.
- Get a hobby: Find something you enjoy that can take your mind off of work for a few hours.
- Practice prayer and mindfulness: Learn how to slow down and recenter your thoughts.
- Create routines to signal to your brain that work is over: Whether it's listening to music on the commute home or walking your dog after work, find something that helps shift your mindset out of work mode.
- Focus on others: Find ways to turn your attention to and help others, which will have the added benefit of taking your mind off of your own work worries.

Once kept in check to prevent it from being a runaway train, that tendency to constantly "work at" things in your mind can lead to a high level of conscientiousness, thoughtfulness, and thoroughness in your work (see Figure 6.1).

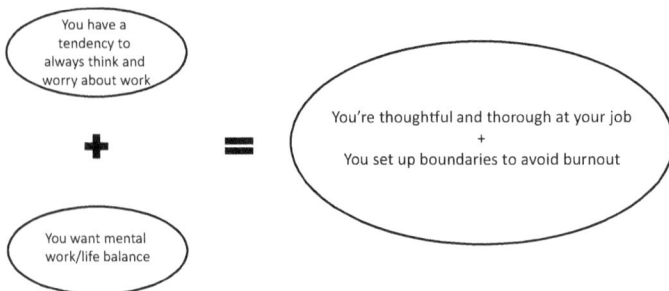

Figure 6.1 Example of how a tendency to constantly worry about work can be turned into a strength

PART 2

Coping With Stress and Anxiety

So far in this book, we've discussed specific challenges, along with methods for mitigating those challenges. While each issue we deal with in life will have its own unique mitigation steps, it's also important to have general methods for coping with stress and anxiety, which can help with multiple challenges that might arise in your life.

In this section, we'll cover three topics:

1. Setting Boundaries and Striking a Balance
2. Developing Your Toolkit of Stress-Relief Techniques
3. Owning Your Challenges

CHAPTER 7

Setting Boundaries and Striking a Balance

When I think of the times I've been at my lowest, it's usually been a time in my life when there was too much going on. When we get overloaded, our batteries get drained, and we don't have time to recharge them. When my batteries are drained, I have a harder time maintaining the defenses and techniques that keep all of the anxiety and negativity in my brain at bay. When that happens, I've found that it's important to stop, review the situation, and see what boundaries I can put in place to keep myself from being overloaded. It's often about trying to find that elusive work/life balance that we hear about. Sometimes even small things can make a difference.

Each situation will be unique. So, rather than keeping things generic, let's look at a couple of specific examples. In the chapter on Observation 6 ("Relaxation? What's That?"), we covered some examples of ways to set boundaries to give your brain a break from thinking about work constantly. In this chapter, we'll discuss examples related to other topics.

Example 1: Business Travel (aka Constant Togetherness)

Before the COVID pandemic shut things down, I used to travel a lot as part of my job. Most of that travel was overseas. And most of that travel was with a group of people. We would often travel as a leadership team, so I would be traveling with my boss and peers.

I'm an extreme introvert. As discussed in the chapter on Observation 1 ("Talking to People is Stressful"), that means that I get my energy from time alone, and being around people drains my batteries. But these

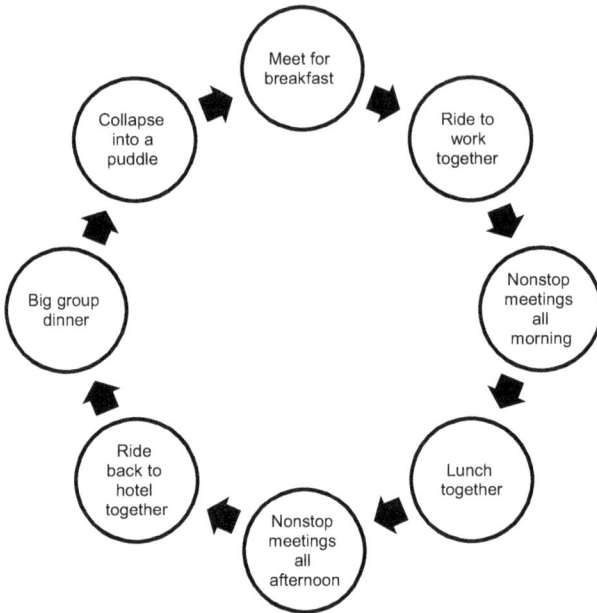

Figure 7.1 A typical day of business travel

business trips were an exercise in constant togetherness, starting with arrival at the airport since we would usually be on the same flights.

These trips would usually be 1 to 2 weeks long and would involve visiting multiple company sites, spending 2 or 3 days at each site, meeting with the local teams. Our agenda during that time is depicted in Figure 7.1 and basically felt like *Groundhog Day*, with each day being pretty much the same:

1. Meet for breakfast in the hotel restaurant
2. Ride to work together
3. Nonstop meetings all morning
4. Lunch together
5. Nonstop meetings all afternoon
6. Ride back to the hotel together
7. Hours-long group dinner with the local team
8. Collapse into a puddle upon returning to my hotel room
9. Repeat the next day

This was not good for my mental health. It gave me no downtime to recharge my batteries. I was with people **all the time**. When not traveling, I might be in meetings and around people all day, but at the end of the day, I could go home and recharge. When traveling, it was nonstop togetherness. We moved together as a herd. I felt like the only time I had to myself was when I went to the bathroom (so I took **lots** of bathroom breaks) or was asleep. It was wearing me down, and putting me in a bad place mentally. I would dread the trips and start stressing about them days in advance. When I got to the airport, I would hope that I wouldn't be arriving at the same time as anyone else, so that I could get through security unseen and find a place to sit alone in the airport until it was time to board. I was looking for anything that would delay the beginning of all of that togetherness.

And the thing is, I **liked** the people I worked with and valued my relationships with them. My co-workers weren't the problem and weren't doing anything wrong. I just couldn't handle the almost complete absence of alone time. I was trying to be a team player and do everything that everyone else was doing, but it caused me to be stressed and more and more worn down as the trip went on. As a result, I wasn't at my best and I'm sure I seemed like a grumpy curmudgeon to my co-workers (which is something else that I would stress about, making things even worse).

What Could I Do Differently?

It finally got to the point where I realized I couldn't keep going without making a change. So, I stepped back and asked myself, "What can I do differently?" I realized that balance was key. I couldn't totally withdraw. These site visits were part of my job. Sure, I could visit the sites on my own, but then I would miss out on valuable conversations that were happening with the leadership team and also miss out on valuable opportunities to build relationships with my boss and peers.

While I couldn't totally withdraw, I could create healthy boundaries. I made a list of what was included on the agenda of our typical days to see what was realistic for me to change. I came up with two possibilities.

First, I could skip meeting everyone for breakfast. I always thought that was crazy anyway. "We're about to spend all day together and you want to spend **even more** time together by meeting for breakfast?" I only did it because I didn't want to seem antisocial. So, I started packing breakfast bars and eating in my room. That would give me a little extra valuable time to myself before the day started.

I also decided I didn't need to go to dinner with the group **every** night. I could occasionally allow myself to have room service or eat someplace alone (usually a fast-food place; I still find eating at a "table service" restaurant by myself to be awkward). The policy I eventually established was that I would go out to dinner once at every site we visited. We usually only spent two or three nights at a site before moving on to the next one, so that meant that I would be available for one big dinner with the local team and then follow it up with a night to myself. If there was a third night there, I would play it by ear but often would be sufficiently recovered to go out with the team again. These occasional nights to myself made a tremendous difference in my ability to maintain my mental health when traveling.

Transparency

One of the keys to putting boundaries in place was being transparent.

First, I had to be transparent with myself that I needed the break and the alone time. I had to acknowledge that it was a true need and not just something I should tough out and fight through.

Second, I needed to be transparent with my boss and my co-workers, so that my need for alone time wasn't being interpreted negatively and harming my relationships with them (and my career).

Before I started being transparent about it, I would try to do everything on these trips but would occasionally reach a breaking point and feel a panicked need to skip a dinner so that I could have some time to myself. I would make up some excuse ("not feeling well" was common and had the benefit of not being untrue) and then spend the entire evening stressing about whether I had offended anyone and whether I had made a mistake. I, therefore, wouldn't really have the relaxing evening I needed, because my stressing about whether I had done the right thing removed some of my ability to recharge.

Eventually, I decided to just talk with my boss about it and ask her if I could take the "one dinner at each site" approach. I explained that it was something that I needed for my mental health. I was pretty stressed about discussing it with her, because I didn't want to seem weak or limited. I imagined being chastised, with a "Well, if you can't handle the demands of the job, we'll just find someone who can."

But the opposite happened. She was immediately supportive. I was fortunate to work for a boss and a company that valued diversity at its core, recognizing that diversity isn't just about the things we can see but also inner character traits. Encouraging and accommodating all kinds of diversity includes recognizing the diversity of personality traits, such as the difference between an extrovert and an introvert. Once I spoke up and was transparent, it was encouraging to hear that I was going to receive support in accommodating my needs as an extreme introvert.

I didn't just discuss it with my boss, but I started being more open with my peers, explaining that I needed extra time to recharge and would be skipping some outings when we traveled. That way I didn't have to stress about how my absence would be interpreted. Not only were my peers supportive, they weren't exactly surprised, and I think they respected the transparency more than my previous method of making up lame excuses to skip things.

I also became comfortable being transparent about this with everyone, even people I barely knew. When we would visit a site, there were usually dinners planned with the local team each night. Maybe I would go to the dinner on the first night and plan to skip dinner on the second night. During that second day, I would have multiple people come by asking, "I hear you're not going to dinner with us tonight? Is everything OK?" I became comfortable explaining that "I've found I need some downtime to maintain my mental health, so I'll be taking a break this evening." One benefit of this transparency was that it turned out to be helpful to other introverts in the organization. I had a number of people tell me how encouraging it was to hear a senior leader discuss this sort of thing so openly and to show it's OK to set boundaries.

I found the practice of being transparent with myself and others to be freeing. Previously, I had effectively been attempting to keep my introverted nature a secret, trying to pretend to be "normal" (in other words, trying to behave like an extrovert). But that practice was unhealthy and just led to more anxiety. Once I was transparent about the reality of being an introvert, I was free to manage it in a way that was healthy for me.

Making these changes resulted in business trips being much more manageable for me. While they were still exhausting, the level of stress and dread decreased because I was able to set boundaries to maintain my mental health. As a result, my performance and contributions on those trips increased, meaning setting these boundaries was not only a benefit to me but to my company.

Example 2: Endless Meetings

My job was a never-ending stream of meetings. Project status reviews. Operations reviews. Staff meetings. Strategy meetings. Governance meetings. Financial reviews. One-on-one meetings. Etcetera, etcetera, etcetera.

I let my calendar control me. I would let every day be completely filled with these meetings. I would have meetings from 8 am until 5 pm (or longer). And then of course I would have a day's worth of emails and other work waiting for me to start working on after meetings ended for the day.

I was accommodating of every request. "Bill wants to talk with me tomorrow, and my day is already full? I guess I can skip lunch and meet with him at noon. Or I can start my day earlier and meet with him at 7:30am. See what works best for him."

Taking this approach was wearing me down and gave me no time to recharge (or get work done). I finally realized that I needed to make a change. This realization occurred at an offsite meeting with my boss and my peers. As part of this meeting, my boss wanted to go around the room and have everyone say one thing they were going to commit to doing the next year to improve their work/life balance. What a great thing to do, right? Who doesn't want a boss who emphasizes the importance of work/life balance? Instead, it kind of ticked me off. I was working so many hours, with no end in sight, that the thought of being asked to "commit" to doing something in my personal life was stressful. It felt like just one more to-do. I wanted to say, "Reduce my workload, and I'll be happy to make a work/life balance commitment."

As we went around the table, each person sharing their commitments in turn, my peers were sharing all kinds of great things that they were going to do. Catch all of their kid's soccer games. Take a vacation they've been putting off. Get back into that yoga class they dropped out of. There were lots of smiles and nods as everyone encouraged each other regarding their ideas. What a nice bonding moment, right? Then we got to me. With reluctance, I said something along the lines of, "I don't know. I guess I'll commit to making it home in time to have dinner with my family two times a week." I'm sure I said it with an air of annoyance. Of course, it was a bizarre answer, because it was setting such a low bar, similar to if I had said I would commit to going home after work and sleeping in my own bed at night. I don't think anyone in the room knew what to do with such a negative answer to what had been a positive exercise, so they just moved on after a moment of awkward silence. Way to bring the room down, dude.

Afterward, I felt a little embarrassed and apologized to my boss. But it served as a wakeup call that my head was in the wrong place and I needed to make a change.

What Could I Do Differently? (aka the "Six Hour" Rule)

I decided that I needed to take control of my calendar. I realized that my calendar was there to support me, not vice versa.

I made the decision to limit myself to 6 hours of meetings per day. Ideally, I would try to limit my "meeting times" to 9 am to 12 pm and 1 pm to 4 pm. By doing so, I had time in the morning to get ready for the day, time at lunch to recharge my batteries, and time at the end of the day to catch up and wrap up.

Obviously, flexibility is important. Not every day can follow my preferred pattern. There were plenty of early and late meetings. But when that happened, I would try to free up another hour in the day, so that I was keeping my meeting time to 6 hours for the day.

And when Bill requested time on my calendar for the next day, when I already had 6 hours of meetings scheduled? The first question was whether it was really urgent or could wait for another day. Most of the time, things can wait. If it was truly urgent, then of course I would talk with him the next day. But that meant one of the other meetings I already had scheduled needed to be pushed out or canceled.

Trying to follow this "6 hour" rule also forced me to re-evaluate which meetings I attended. I started asking more critical questions about the meetings on my calendar. Are there meetings that I could skip or delegate to someone else? Are there regular meetings that are needed but could be reduced in frequency or length? Are people scheduling meetings for an hour that could be 30 minutes? When I have a conflict with a regular meeting (like a weekly one-on-one), does it need to be rescheduled or could we just cancel that week's occurrence?

There were days when I couldn't follow my "6 hour" rule because there were just too many important things going on. The key was to make those days the exception, not the rule.

This approach protected my mental health and prevented burn-out. It also allowed me to be fully present in the meetings I attended. I enjoy and value connecting with people, and I can do that more effectively when I'm able to recharge my batteries.

A Note on Work/Life Balance

We've all heard the motivational sayings. "When on their death bed, no one wishes they had spent more time at work." "In twenty years, the only people who will remember that you worked late are your family." And I agree with those things whole-heartedly. The concept of family and faith being a higher priority than work is a core value for me. But the question is, how do I turn those motivational sayings into action?

It comes down to the topic of this chapter: setting boundaries and striking a balance. And it won't happen by accident. You have to make conscious decisions regarding what boundaries to set and be disciplined in following through.

Some of the examples provided in this chapter and in the chapter on Observation 6 helped me with my work/life balance. The decision to limit my meetings to 6 hours per day helped me get home earlier. I described in Chapter 6 how I protected my weekends. I would work however many hours I needed to Monday through Friday but had a rule of never working on the weekend (absent a true emergency popping up, of course). And the practice I described in Chapter 6 of always taking all of my Paid Time Off certainly helped with work/life balance.

There were other boundaries I established. When my son was young and playing various sports, I left work in time to attend his games no matter what was going on. I planned lots of activities with my kids and considered those "calendar appointments" to be about as unmissable as a meeting with the CEO.

When I wrote my first book, I had a 9-year-old son, a newborn, and a demanding job. It probably wasn't the best time to be taking on the extra work of writing a book, but we can't always control the timing of opportunities. I decided that this was a case where I needed to set boundaries, both to make sure I got the book done but also to make sure I didn't de-prioritize my family. For the months that I was writing the first draft, I placed a series of 2-hour writing sessions on the family calendar each week. When it was time for those sessions, I wrote for 2 hours. I wouldn't let myself write for more time or less time than that. With this process, I knew I was making progress on the book but also that I wasn't going overboard. And my family knew exactly what to expect. They knew when I'd be unavailable versus me just randomly disappearing on them throughout the writing process.

The point is that you have to make what you might call "Work/Life Balance Resolutions," making sure they're practical and actionable, and then follow through on them.

It's not always easy. And some jobs make it nearly impossible. I've always had a strong work ethic. I considered my job to be a gift from God, and I wanted to be a good steward of that gift. So, I was going to do whatever it took to do that job well. But if I couldn't do so without maintaining a healthy work/life balance, something needed to change. Usually that's when I realized I needed to set boundaries (and/or find ways to work more efficiently). Ultimately, if I couldn't find a way to do so, it would have been time for a job change (but fortunately it never came to that for me).

Why am I spending so much time talking about work/life balance in a section of the book about managing stress and anxiety? Because when you make a decision to set boundaries to protect your work/life balance, develop a specific plan for doing so, and follow through on that plan, it can have the added impact of reducing stress and anxiety. It will give you that time you need to recharge your batteries. And it will reduce the stress and guilt that come with feeling that you're not spending enough time on the things that are important to you.

Summary

We all have times in our lives when we feel overwhelmed, and it's important in those times to step back and identify opportunities for setting boundaries. It's a fact of life that companies will take as much from us as we're willing to give. Even the best companies will let you work nonstop if you insist on doing so. But only the worst companies **expect** you to do so. It's up to us to establish boundaries to protect our mental health and work/life balance.

Each situation will be unique. The examples in this chapter can hopefully help spur some thought, but you have to take time and do the analysis to determine what might help in your specific circumstance. Remember that even little things can help, both in relieving the pressure and also helping you feel you have some control over the situation. The key is to intentionally explore what opportunities you have to set healthy boundaries.

CHAPTER 8

Developing Your Toolkit of Stress-Relief Techniques

Part 1 of this book was dedicated to describing techniques for mitigating specific challenges (such as fear of public speaking). While those targeted techniques are critical for addressing our most common challenges, it's also important to have a toolkit of stress-relief techniques that you can go to on a regular basis, when dealing with new situations or just feeling general stress and anxiety. The techniques listed in this chapter are broader in nature than those targeted techniques covered in earlier chapters (although there is some overlap, as some of these "broader" items are also ones that I use to help mitigate my most common issues).

I look at it as a toolkit. "I'm feeling stressed. Which item in my toolkit can I pull out to help me with this situation?" We'll cover eight items that I've placed in my personal toolkit:

- Breathing Exercises
- Posture
- Exercise
- Self-talk
- Mindfulness
- Prayer
- Counseling and Therapy
- Mentoring and Coaching

These are the techniques that I've found helpful to me over the years. You likely already have your own toolkit, but hopefully you'll find one or more things here that you can add. You probably have some things in your toolkit that I could learn from too. So, grab some time on my calendar, and we'll compare notes. (But don't really. Because of the whole social anxiety thing.)

My Toolkit

Breathing Exercises

In Part 1 of this book, we discussed breathing techniques as mitigation tools, both related to fear of public speaking and to stress resulting from speaking up in large meetings. I've found that these techniques help settle me down in just about any stressful situation. I'm in the middle of something that's stressing me out? I'll take a few seconds to focus on my breathing. I'm about to enter a stressful situation? I'll spend some time proactively focusing on my breathing before it starts.

I find that these breathing exercises help me feel more alert and calm me down. With some adept googling, you can find multiple studies describing how these sorts of breathing exercises can signal "relaxation" to your brain.[1] But I didn't start because I read a bunch of studies. My therapist recommended I give it a try and it worked, so I added it to my toolkit.

The breathing technique I use is called 4-7-8 breathing:

- Breathe in through your nose for 4 seconds
- Hold the breath for 7 seconds
- Exhale through your mouth for 8 seconds

I generally would do this two to three times at the beginning of any work day and another two to three times either right before or during stressful meetings.

Another common breathing technique is called box breathing, which is similar to 4-7-8 breathing except with different lengths of time:

- Breathe in through your nose for 4 seconds
- Hold the breath for 4 seconds
- Exhale through your mouth for 4 seconds
- Hold your breath again for 4 seconds

Why do I choose 4-7-8 breathing over box breathing? Simply because it's the first one I tried and it worked. I have no reason to believe one is better than the other. I think you'll find that either one is helpful in calming your mind down.[*]

Posture

Earlier in this book, I discussed how focusing on posture helps me both in giving presentations and in speaking up when in big meetings. Before I start a presentation, I spend a couple of minutes with my shoulders back and feet apart, and then I make sure I maintain a "broad" posture throughout the presentation. When sitting in big meetings, I'll similarly sit at the table in an upright posture, shoulders back and legs apart. Basically, I try to make myself big and broad, because I find it increases my confidence and decreases my stress, while also helping me feel more alert.

I learned about this concept by watching Amy Cuddy's excellent TED Talk about how body language shapes who you are.[2] Watching her talk was 20 minutes well spent and is highly recommended.

I won't attempt to duplicate her talk here or go too far in summarizing it. But think about when people are feeling powerful. They tend to make themselves big, such as spreading their arms out in celebration when crossing the finish line of a race. And when people are feeling powerless, they tend to fold up and make themselves small. Cuddy and her team's studies indicated that these poses can actually lead to hormonal changes, with high-power poses (such as the image on the right side of Figure 8.1) increasing confidence and decreasing stress and low-power poses (such as the image on the left side of Figure 8.1) doing the opposite. In other words, if you pretend to be powerful, you're more likely to feel powerful.

---

[*]Dr. Andrew Weil is commonly credited with developing the 4-7-8 breathing technique. Former Navy SEAL Mark Divine is commonly credited with naming and popularizing the box breathing technique.

Figure 8.1 **Examples of low-power and high-power poses**

I found that adapting these techniques (making myself "big" or, in Cuddy's terms, adopting a high-power pose) indeed had a positive impact on my confidence level in stressful situations.[†]

Exercise

For the first 15 years or so of my career, I attempted various workout plans. I rotated between the couch potato and slug plans, and even dabbled in the ne'er-do-well conditioning program for a while. Then, I decided that I should consider adding actual exercise to my routine, and it was a game changer. For the last twenty-ish years of my career, I got up early so that I could take a brisk walk for 30 minutes before going to work (nothing extreme; just enough to build up a sweat).

I found that this 30 minute investment helped me start the day feeling more alert and less stressed.

While I love a good walk outside, my morning walk is usually on a treadmill, just because it makes it easier for me to be consistent with my speed and incline and for me to push myself to work up a sweat. Plus, it gives me time to watch TV shows that I wouldn't otherwise have time for. I've watched many TV series from the treadmill, one episode per morning. What better way to start your work day than with an episode of *Breaking Bad* or *Buffy the Vampire Slayer*? And when I would

[†]Original art for Figure 8.1 by Alan Pickett of Alan T Pickett Art Studios.

take those stressful work trips that I mentioned in the previous chapter? I'd do my morning walk outside (assuming we were someplace where it was safe to do so), which would have the dual benefit of reducing stress before the start of a difficult day and also giving me the opportunity to explore a new place.

Similar to the discussion on breathing techniques, there's some science stuff behind all of this and how exercise can help anxiety, if you're inclined to look into it.[3] But I do it because it works for me.

Self-Talk (aka "Be Nice to Yourself")

We covered self-talk in detail in the chapter on Observation 5 ("Everyone (Else) is Awesome"). As a reminder, I described my tendency to say "I hate myself" and other similarly not-so-helpful things and how I attempt to redirect those thoughts, preferably by replacing them with more positive thoughts or at the very least halting the flow of negative comments. As tempting as it is to run up the word count on this book by doing a giant "copy and paste" of that section here (hoping you won't notice), I'll instead refer you back to that chapter if you'd like a refresher on that discussion.

From a general stress-relief toolkit standpoint, I've found it's helpful to save positive notes and feedback I've received from others, whether in electronic form or hardcopy, and have those available for easy access when I'm feeling down. When I used to travel frequently for work, I had a particularly sweet note from my daughter that I carried with me. It's one of the best-traveled pieces of paper in history. When I start feeling down about myself, I can re-read those notes as a way to remind myself that I'm not all bad and to build myself back up.

Mindfulness

I considered not including this one, not because I don't believe in its benefits, but because I feel like a hypocrite. I'm not good at it, and it's the item in my toolkit that I use least often. It's like that giant flat-head screwdriver that only fits the most ginormous of screws but you keep around "just in case," gathering dust in the bottom of your toolbox.

If you're not familiar with the term, mindfulness is about being fully present in the moment and not letting your mind wander to other thoughts. It's a good technique for centering yourself and getting your mind to stop spinning. It can be something as simple as focusing solely on your breathing, not letting yourself think about anything except the process of breathing in and out. Or it can be a focus on various parts of your body and releasing tension from them. I honestly have a hard time staying focused on it. I get bored and my mind wanders. Some people listen to audio to help them relax and focus, with a speaker telling them what to do, in their best ASMR voice. ("Breathe in through your nose. Notice the feeling of the breath in your nostrils. Feel the breath as it travels down your throat and into your lungs. Breathe out. Feel the rush of air as it's expelled from your body.") I tried that and just couldn't do it. I found the guide voice to be annoying, not soothing. And I couldn't get past my own self-consciousness. When my counselor introduced me to it, she tried to walk me through the exercise in her office. She had me close my eyes as she guided me through focusing on my breathing and then on releasing the tension in various muscles and body parts. I did manage to fully achieve mindfulness, if we define mindfulness as being mindful that someone was watching me as I attempted mindfulness. I was way too self-conscious for it to succeed in that setting. It was purely an endurance exercise. I even felt self-conscious trying to do it on my own in an empty room as part of my homework.

Despite my failings with this tool, there are a lot of people who benefit from mindfulness exercises, and I think the concept of focusing the mind to quiet the nonstop barrage of anxieties is a good one. It's just something that I've struggled with. I include it here because I believe it's something worth exploring.

There is one very simple application of mindfulness that I've used with some success. If I'm really stressing about something, usually taking my dog for a walk outside, with my headphones on and listening to music, is a great way to take my mind off of it. But there are times when I'm so stressed that I can't even get myself to focus on the music. In those cases, I find it works if I turn the music off and just focus on counting my steps, starting over each time I get to 10. "1, 2, 3, 4, 5, 6,

7, 8, 9, 10. 1, 2, 3, 4, 5, 6, 7, 8, 9, 10." This will force my mind into focus and away from whatever stress I'm fixated on.

One reason I probably haven't tried harder to develop my mindfulness skills is that if I'm going to sit and quiet my mind, I'm likely to focus on the next item on this list instead of on mindfulness (not that the two are mutually exclusive).

Prayer

It's amazing to me how often the following scenario plays out:

- I'm stressed about something. It could be I'm worried about something that might happen. It could be I'm beating myself up about something I did and wondering how to make things right. It could be that I'm trying to figure out how to resolve a stressful problem. Regardless, my head is spinning, and the anxiety is wearing me out.
- I spend time praying about it.
- In the midst of that prayer, I get ideas about how to handle the situation and a feeling for the best path to take.
- I end the prayer feeling more at peace and with a direction.

Is that God speaking to me and helping me with the problem I'm bringing to Him? Or is it just my own brain working through the problem as I sit and focus on it? My guess is that sometimes it's one and sometimes it's the other and sometimes it's a combination. But the bottom line is that it works.[‡]

[‡]For those who have a "religion is the opiate of the masses" viewpoint of these things and are inclined to dismiss this item, I'll just say that I'm not a "blind faith" type of person and need concrete reasons for believing what I believe. I'm also not a Biblical scholar or a theologian, but after spending some time looking into it, I ultimately decided that believing in the tenets of the Christian faith was more logical than any other answer. If it's something you have interest in exploring, the resources that were most helpful to me were *Mere Christianity* by C.S. Lewis, *I Don't Have Enough Faith to Be an Atheist* by Norman L. Geisler and Frank Turek, *Evidence That Demands a Verdict* by Josh McDowell and Sean McDowell, and the *Hacks for Life with Galon Jones* podcast.

Of course, I try to make sure my prayers aren't just about requests for help with my specific problems. I find that prayer in general (whether it's prayers of thanks or requests for others or what-have-you) helps me feel more at peace. It can help me to focus on positives (things to be grateful for) and on the needs of others.

Counseling and Therapy

I grew up in a generation that viewed seeing a therapist as a sign of weakness, at least for men. Dealing with stress? Struggling with depression? Reeling from grief? Suck it up, rub some dirt on it, and get back out there! So, I went through most of my life not really even considering counseling and therapy as a possibility, regardless of what issues I was dealing with. I mean, I should just be strong and fight through it, right?

But if you had a broken arm, would you try to manage it on your own? Would you say, "Seeing a doctor is weak. I'll just deal with it myself and hope it heals"? No, you'd go see a doctor and have your arm set, because you'd want it to heal as quickly and effectively as possible. Well, your mental health is more important than your arm, so why would you be hesitant to get help with it? That thought process helped me get past the stigma that was embedded in my brain.

A few years ago, everything caught up to me. A combination of things (work stress, health issues, and constant travel between time zones, to name a few) had me in a place I had never been before. My mental defenses were down, and the barrage of negativity in my head was constant. The avalanche of anxiety and self-loathing was more than I wanted to keep dealing with, and for the first time in life, I wondered whether I wanted to keep going (which fortunately never went beyond a "thought"). I was miserable, and my wife could clearly see that something was wrong. She encouraged me to get help. I found a good counselor and spent a few weeks learning techniques to mitigate the anxiety and stress I was dealing with. I still use many of those techniques to this day, and you've read about some of them in this book.

That's the most serious concern I've seen a counselor about, but there have been others, such as the time when fears and anxieties were preventing me from being able to sleep whenever I was in a hotel room by myself. Given how much I traveled for work, that was a fun time. Again, I saw someone for a few weeks until I felt like I had some tools to redirect my thoughts in those situations.

The point is, sometimes we have issues and need to see someone who's trained to help us deal with those issues. Sometimes they're physical health issues and sometimes they're mental health issues. There are specialists who can help us deal with both. I've become a big believer in the benefit of therapy and counseling in helping with those mental health issues.[§]

It seems like on TV and in the movies, the way it works is that people have their therapist, and they go see that person every single week, indefinitely. That's certainly one approach to it, and that's great if you get ongoing value from it and it helps keep you on the right track. For me, I guess I've treated it more like I do physical therapy. In the past, I've had hip and wrist injuries, and recovery from those injuries required physical therapy. I saw a physical therapist regularly for a while. They would give me specific exercises to work on between sessions so that I could heal and get stronger, and then when we got together, we could measure my progress. Once I reached a certain point of progress in my healing, I didn't need to see the physical therapist anymore, and I could continue to work on my maintenance exercises on my own. If I had a setback, I could go back and see them, but otherwise there was no need.

That's how I've treated counseling and therapy. As I described earlier, there have been times when my anxiety has gotten the best of me, and I realized I needed help. I would see a counselor for a while to get help getting back on the right track, until I felt I was in a healthier place and had good tools to stay in that healthier place. How would I know when I was "ready" to stop the sessions? As with a physical therapist, it

---

[§]For the purposes of this discussion, I'm using therapy and counseling pretty much interchangeably. There are differences, although trying to find a clear consensus on the definitions will give you tired-head. In general, counseling tends to refer to shorter-term, more goal-oriented advice, while therapy tends to refer to a longer-term focus on underlying mental health issues. Based on that interpretation, I've personally always focused on counseling (in other words, treating a specific issue).

was based on a combination of how I was feeling and input from my counselor.

Again, you might decide that having a "permanent" therapist that you see on a regular basis indefinitely is the right thing for you. I just take a more task and objective-oriented approach. "I have a problem. I'm going to see an expert to help me address that problem. And when I feel that problem has been adequately addressed, I'll stop." I do have a "regular" counselor, just like I have a "regular" doctor. And just like my doctor, I don't see her every week. I see her when I have an issue.[¶] That's not the only way to do it, but it's worked for me. The point is, deciding to get counseling doesn't have to be like what you see on TV—it doesn't mean that you'll be adding it to your calendar (and your expenses) every week for the rest of your life, unless that's how you decide you want to do it.

Mentoring and Coaching

While counseling and therapy have their place, it's amazing how therapeutic it can be to just sit down with a trusted advisor and share the things that are causing me stress and anxiety. Just the act of talking through the details, and having someone listen to them, helps ease the stress. But then getting the other person's perspective and advice can help form a plan for how to deal with the situation (or sometimes help with the realization that there's no "situation" to deal with).

Sometimes you need to talk with and get advice from someone who's not in your "chain of command." For example, my mind has a tendency to spin out of control if I think I've made a mistake, whether in my work or in my interactions with a co-worker. I certainly didn't want to bother my boss every time I was having an anxiety attack over something, because I didn't want to develop a reputation as a high-maintenance employee. But I needed to talk with someone to help get my mind unstuck. Over the years, I developed a short list of people that I trusted and who I would go to when in those situations. Some of them were former bosses (in other words, more formal mentors),

---

[¶] Yes, I do see my doctor for an annual physical too, and I don't do that with my counselor. All analogies break down at some point.

and some of them were peers and friends. Because, in my experience, mentoring and coaching is something that the right peers and friends can provide for each other. Today, you might provide mentoring and coaching for me, and tomorrow I might do the same for you.

Some companies have formal mentoring programs, where you can be "matched" with someone who's further along in their career and who can not only provide career advice but also situational advice, such as if you're dealing with a particularly stressful situation. I served in the role of mentor in those sorts of programs for many years, and I was happy to be a "safe space" for people to discuss situations they were in that were causing them anxiety. I could listen, provide perspective, and help brainstorm on an approach. The "perspective" part is critical. In my experience, we pretty frequently get spun up about things that really aren't that big of a deal, and an objective third party can help us see that.

If your company has a formal mentoring program, it's worth looking into participating in it so that you can be matched with a mentor. If it doesn't, consider identifying one on your own, either by leveraging your contacts or asking your boss to help you. If nothing else, it's helpful to identify your trusted advisors (which could just be the right peers and friends) who can be your go-to people when you need to talk something out.

There are also situations where a formal coach can help (in other words, someone who's paid to be a professional coach). When discussing counseling and therapy, I mentioned that I used that tool when wanting help with a specific issue I was struggling with (versus having a "permanent" ongoing therapist that I saw indefinitely). There are times when instead a paid coach can be the right answer to help you overcome a specific anxiety-related challenge. For example, if you're trying to overcome a fear of public speaking, a public speaking coach might be the right answer instead of a counselor. Or if you're trying to improve your ability to form relationships at work and overcome your social anxiety, a professional coach who can help you develop relationship-building tactics and techniques could be helpful. I personally have never paid for a professional coach out of my own pocket, but I did make use of some coaching resources that my company made available.

Your company's human resources or training departments might have coaching resources available to help.

A Note About What's Not Included in This List

After a close friend read the first draft of this book, he commented that it seemed like a glaring omission that I didn't mention anything about anxiety medications in this list of stress-relief techniques, since pharmaceuticals are so commonly prescribed for anxiety. My initial reaction was that this is my personal toolkit, and I never used anxiety medication. So, that topic didn't belong on this list. But upon further reflection, I decided that it does seem odd not to mention it.

Bottom line, I'm not a doctor and this book isn't the place for advice regarding medications. While I've personally never used medications to help with anxiety, I know plenty of people who have. Some of them swear by those medications and feel that they've improved their quality of life. Others have stopped taking the medications because they weren't comfortable with the side effects. If this is something you're interested in exploring, conversations with your doctor and/or your therapist are a good place to start.

As far as why I personally didn't choose to take medications to help with my anxiety, ironically anxiety was a big factor. As someone who worked at a job where my success was all about the sharpness of my mind, I had anxiety about taking anything that changed how my brain functioned. And I felt like the techniques described throughout this book were working for me. Maybe that approach led to things being a lot harder than they needed to be, but it was the choice I was personally most comfortable with.

The stress-relief techniques described in this chapter can be used independent of or in conjunction with any anxiety-related medication you choose to add to your toolkit.

Summary

We all need to build a toolkit of stress-relief techniques. Life puts us in situations that cause anxiety, and we might not have developed the perfect method for mitigating that specific anxiety. That's when it's important to have go-to tools to help.

In this chapter, we covered eight potential tools for your toolkit:

- Breathing Exercises
- Posture
- Exercise
- Self-talk
- Mindfulness
- Prayer
- Counseling and Therapy
- Mentoring and Coaching

The key is to figure out which ones work for you, identify any additional tools you like to use that weren't covered in this chapter, and then practice using them so that you're ready when they're needed.

CHAPTER 9

Owning Your Challenges

I went through a large portion of my career pretending to be something I wasn't. I was a leader at my company, and I felt like I needed to project strength. People needed to have confidence in me. How were they going to do that if I admitted that I struggled with social anxiety and an inferiority complex? Better to keep those things to myself, right?

There is certainly some wisdom to that. I couldn't lead people if the image I was projecting was "basket case". I had to mitigate those challenges and overcome them in order to do my job effectively. That's what the majority of this book is about.

But a funny thing happened as I got further along in my career and more comfortable in my own skin and with my accomplishments. I found that I no longer cared if people knew what my internal struggles were. I leaned more and more into just being transparent.

Before I could be transparent with others though, I had to first be transparent with myself. In some cases, it was a long time before I realized (or at least was willing to admit to myself) that I struggled with certain anxieties. I spent a lot of time compensating for them on a purely subconscious level. Becoming more self-aware was a journey, one that was aided both by counseling and also just time and maturity.

One of the most powerful things in life is the ability to help others who are going through something that we've gone through. We've all seen it. A friend is going through a trauma (maybe the loss of a close family member or being diagnosed with an illness), and no one is in a better position to help them than a person who has gone through the same thing. My heart might be breaking for them and I can try to say the right things and be there for them, but I don't really know what they're going through so I can't speak from experience. That person who has dealt with the same thing can help them in a way that I can't. They will be able to empathize and share experience and advice that can only come from having "been there."

Once I got more comfortable with understanding and being transparent about my challenges, I was surprised to discover just how many of my co-workers dealt with the same things. Because I had spent years dealing with and mitigating those things in a corporate setting, I was in a position to share what had worked for me and to help others as they forged their own paths. I like to think that I became a "safe space" for other anxiety-filled introverts to discuss their challenges, and I hope I was able to provide some helpful counsel. A lot of those conversations were in one-on-one settings, but I also did some presentations on the topic to larger groups. I thought it was important for people to know that senior leaders in the company struggled with these things too.

And it's not a one-way street. Being transparent about your challenges doesn't just put you in position to help others who are dealing with similar things. It puts others in a position to help you. In those conversations I had with others, I received valuable tips and advice that helped me and that I never would have received if I hadn't been willing to open up. And it helped me feel like I had a support system when I was at work, with others I could go to when I needed advice or just needed to talk to someone who would understand.

Owning Your Challenges ≠ Making Excuses

It's critical to understand that owning your challenges doesn't mean that you wallow in them or use them as an excuse. We all have performance expectations, and we all have behavior expectations. It's my responsibility to live up to those expectations, regardless of what anxieties I might be feeling. If my job requires me to give presentations, I can't say to my boss, "Sorry, I have a fear of public speaking, so I can't do it." My boss would say, "Fine, then you're not the right person for this job." Similarly, I can't say, "Boss, I know I never talk to my co-workers and have no relationship with them. But I have social anxiety, and I'm an introvert, so I can't be expected to talk to people. Sorry." Again, my boss would say, "Communicating with and getting along with your co-workers is part of the job. If you can't do it, then you can't do the job."

But awareness of my challenges puts me in position to mitigate them and, when I fall short, better understand why I fell short and address it.

A Story

A few years ago, I went into a co-worker's office for a regularly-scheduled routine one-on-one. This was a co-worker who was important to my ability to be successful at my job and who I thought I had a strong relationship with. I had no reason to think there was going to be anything different about this meeting as compared to all of our other regular meetings. I figured we'd have some small talk and then catch up on the status of a few tactical items.

Instead, a few minutes into the meeting, this co-worker started giving me some feedback. She told me about things I had been doing recently that frustrated her. The feedback lasted for 45 minutes. It wasn't just about one thing either. It was a laundry list of different things that she was unhappy about. Do you remember that great pop single from the early 80s by The Romantics called "What I Like About You"? Well, this meeting felt like I was hearing a follow-up song called "What I Don't Like About You." Except it wasn't as catchy. And was more of a rock opera or overture, at 45 minutes long.

I had been given plenty of feedback in my career but had never experienced someone giving me so much unexpected feedback and for so long. Fortunately, I was able to fall back on some of the techniques for receiving feedback that we discussed earlier in this book (in the chapter on "Observation 5: Everyone (Else) is Awesome"). I asked clarifying questions to understand the feedback but didn't argue it. I took notes on each of the distinct feedback items I was given and focused on making sure I understood them. But when the meeting ended, I was stunned and shell-shocked on the inside.

When I went home that night, I was feeling low. I sat on the couch in a practically catatonic state. I didn't have the energy to talk or read or watch TV. I really didn't know how to bounce back from it. It's not that the feedback my co-worker had given me wasn't valid and

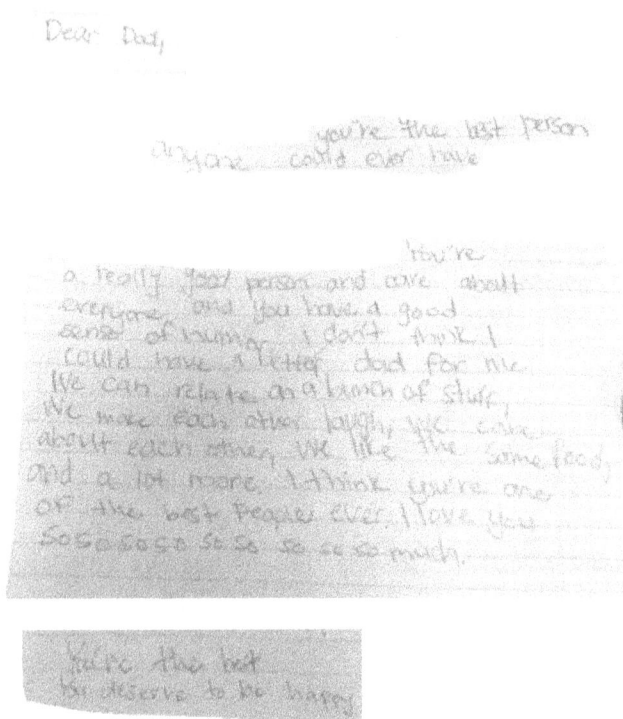

Figure 9.1 The note my daughter left for me after my rough day at work

wasn't important for me to hear. It's just that it was too much at once, especially for someone who already struggles with self-confidence issues.

As I was sitting there in my depressive state, my daughter, who was in her early teens at the time, asked me what was wrong. My initial instinct was to respond with, "Nothing, I'm fine." But she deals with a lot of the same things I do. I thought if anyone could understand why I was so down, it would be her. And I also thought it was good for her to see that others, including her dad, deal with this sort of anxiety too. So, I told her the whole story. She was sweet and empathetic. I didn't really think anything else of it once we finished our discussion. I just went back to my regularly scheduled programming for the evening of feeling depressed.

I didn't sleep well that night. But I got up the next morning at my normal time and dragged myself to my treadmill for my morning exercise routine, still feeling every bit as drained as I had the night before. Waiting there beside the treadmill was a note from my daughter.

I've included an image of that note here (see Figure 9.1), with some parts that were a little too specific to the situation removed.

I'm not embarrassed to say that I teared up when I saw this note. For my daughter to go to bed still worried about me and about how sad I was, and for her to then get up, write this sweet note, and put it in a location where she knew I'd see it first thing in the morning… well, it was incredibly touching. It turned my whole morning around and changed my mindset. Suddenly, my co-worker's feedback didn't seem as important, with the reminder that I had people at home who were more important to me and who thought I was pretty great.

With this renewed energy and perspective, I spent the morning going through my notes from the previous day's feedback marathon. I parsed the feedback into 10 distinct items. For each one, I made a plan for how I was going to address it, with the exception of two items that I either didn't understand or just really didn't agree with. I got on my co-worker's calendar for that afternoon. When we met, I thanked her for the feedback and went through each item one by one. For each, the approach was, "This is what I heard you say. Did I hear that correctly? This is what I plan to do about it." For the two items that I didn't understand or didn't agree with, I asked for clarity. In both cases, she withdrew the feedback after further reflection. It was a positive meeting. I think she appreciated how seriously I took her feedback and my plans to address her concerns, and the experience strengthened our relationship overall.

Summary

So, what was the point of telling that story? It's a real-world example of some of the things we've been discussing in this chapter.

First, being transparent about your struggles sets a good example and helps others. And sets them up to help you. If I hadn't been willing to share why I was down, my daughter wouldn't have been able to help me. And it helps her to know that she's not the only one who gets down because of things that others say and that she has a dad who can relate to her when she does. The point here is to keep an eye out for appropriate opportunities to be transparent and vulnerable with others.

Second, my daughter was able to empathize with me because she deals with a lot of the same things that I do. How many kids would be that thoughtful? But she knows what it's like, so she empathized, was truly concerned, and wanted to do something to help. We covered earlier how one of the most powerful things in life is the ability to help others who are going through something that we've gone through. She knew that what I needed was for someone to build me back up. It's a reminder to always be on the lookout for those people who are dealing with the same challenges as us. We're in a unique position to help them (and be helped by them).

Finally, it was a reminder of what's really important. After reading her note, I remembered that work isn't the most important thing, and it helped me get in the right mindset to address the feedback with less emotion (constructively and without making excuses). No matter what else is going on in my life and no matter what other people might say to me, I have a family that loves me and thinks I'm great. Remember, owning your challenges doesn't mean that you wallow in them or use them as an excuse. Keeping things in perspective, including counting your blessings and remembering what's most important in life, can help not only with your personal happiness but also with having the right mindset when dealing with obstacles.

Conclusion

I'm not a big podcast guy. I tend to listen to music when in the car or when taking a walk. But there are a couple of podcasts that I listen to regularly. One of them is *Office Ladies*, a rewatch podcast for the greatest comedy show of all time (which everyone knows is the U.S. version of *The Office*). One of the podcast's hosts, Jenna Fischer (who played Pam on the show), is very open about her struggles with anxiety. One of the analogies she's used is that anxiety is like a backpack that you always carry with you. Some days the backpack is weighed down with anxieties, and it can be difficult to carry. Some days the backpack is fairly empty so the load is lighter.*

The ideas given in this book are intended to help make your backpack lighter. Remember, your mileage may vary. The techniques that I've described have helped me. If you deal with similar challenges, those same techniques will hopefully help you too. If you deal with different challenges, hopefully reading about those specific coping mechanisms will help spur ideas that will help you develop your own.

The key is to remember:

We all have internal struggles. Even the most successful leader or expert at your company has them.

Don't put artificial limits on yourself because of them.

Be aware of them. Mitigate them so that they don't become derailers. And figure out how that unique perspective and experience can be turned into an advantage.

Doing so will help you not only survive but also thrive in the workplace.

---

* Jenna has mentioned the backpack analogy a few times, but I can't point you to specific episodes where she said it. Because my memory isn't that good. And it exhausts me to think about how to find a specific quote among a billion episodes of a podcast. Just listen to them all. They're good. Jenna also wrote *The Actor's Life: A Survival Guide* (BenBella Books, 2017), which is a guide for aspiring actors. Sort of a "here are the things I wish I had known when I was starting out" kind of a book. Which is what this book is intended to be. Which means that Jenna and I have something in common. Which means we'll probably become fast friends whenever we get around to meeting, and I'll likely be invited to join her and Angela Kinsey as a co-host on their podcast. So, look for that to happen.

Notes

Introduction

1. Goodreads, "Popular Quotes."
2. Walker, "Ted Williams."

Chapter 1

1. Brahm, *The Twilight Zone.*

Chapter 2

1. Zauderer, "31 Fear of Public Speaking Statistics (Prevalence)."; Gaines, "Fool Yourself Out of Your Fear of Public Speaking."

Chapter 3

1. Holland, *The Office.*
2. Collins, *Good to Great: Why Some Companies Make the Leap...And Others Don't.*

Chapter 5

1. Gladwell, *Outliers: The Story of Success.*
2. Saymeh, "What is Imposter Syndrome? Definition, Symptoms, and Overcoming It."
3. Psychology Today, "Imposter Syndrome."
4. Franken, *Saturday Night Live.*
5. Davies, "God's Children."

Chapter 8

1. Seppälä, Bradley, and Goldstein "Research: Why Breathing Is So Effective at Reducing Stress."
2. Cuddy, "Your Body Language May Shape Who You Are."
3. Mayo Clinic, "Depression and Anxiety: Exercise Eases Symptoms."

References

Brahm, John, dir. *The Twilight Zone*. Written by Rod Serling, featuring Burgess Meredith. November 20, 1959; CBS.

Collins, Jim. *Good to Great: Why Some Companies Make the Leap...And Others Don't* (Harper Business, 2001).

Cuddy, Amy. "Your Body Language May Shape Who You Are." Accessed April 4, 2024. www.ted.com/talks/amy_cuddy_your_body_language_may_shape_who_you_are.

Davies, Ray. "God's Children." *Percy* (1971).

Franken, Al. *Saturday Night Live*. 1991; NBC

Gladwell, Malcolm. *Outliers: The Story of Success* (Little, Brown and Company, 2008).

Gaines, Jordan. "Fool Yourself Out of Your Fear of Public Speaking." *NBC News* (2013). Accessed April 4, 2024. www.nbcnews.com/health/body-odd/fool-yourself-out-your-fear-public-speaking-flna1b9522172.

Goodreads. "Popular Quotes." Accessed April 4, 2024. www.goodreads.com/quotes.

Holland, Dean, dir. *The Office*. Written by Jennifer Celotta, featuring Steve Carell and Andy Buckley, January 15, 2009; NBC.

Mayo Clinic. "Depression and Anxiety: Exercise Eases Symptoms." Accessed April 4, 2024. www.mayoclinic.org/diseases-conditions/depression/in-depth/depression-and-exercise/art-20046495.

Psychology Today, "Imposter Syndrome." Accessed April 4, 2024. www.psychologytoday.com/us/basics/imposter-syndrome.

Saymeh, Amal. "What Is Imposter Syndrome? Definition, Symptoms, and Overcoming It." *BetterUp* (2023). Accessed April 4, 2024. www.betterup.com/blog/what-is-imposter-syndrome-and-how-to-avoid-it.

Seppälä, Emma, Christina Bradley, and Michael R. Goldstein. "Research: Why Breathing Is So Effective at Reducing Stress." *Harvard Business Review* (2020). hbr.org/2020/09/research-why-breathing-is-so-effective-at-reducing-stress.

Walker, Steve. "Ted Williams." *Society for American Baseball Research*. Accessed April 4, 2024. https://sabr.org/journal/article/ted-williams.

Zauderer, Steven. "31 Fear of Public Speaking Statistics (Prevalence)." *Cross River Therapy* (2023). Accessed April 4, 2024. www.crossrivertherapy.com/public-speaking-statistics

About the Author

Mike Schiller has more than 30 years of experience at Fortune 500 companies, both as a technical expert and as an executive-level leader, and most recently was vice president and chief information security officer at Texas Instruments. He is currently president of Onward Consulting, LLC, specializing in information security and audit consulting. Mike is a graduate of Texas A&M University, and his previous writing credits include *IT Auditing: Using Controls to Protect Information Assets*. Mike is an **anxiety-filled introvert** and enjoys helping others with similar challenges succeed.

Index

OTHER TITLES IN THE BUSINESS CAREER DEVELOPMENT COLLECTION

Vilma Barr, Consultant, Editor

- *Classroom to Workplace* by Lynn Appelbaum
- *Working in Business and Finance* by Joseph Malgesini
- *Make Your Internship Count* by Marti Fischer
- *Sales Excellence* by Eden White
- *How to Think Strategically* by Greg Githens
- *Succeeding as a Young Entrepreneur* by Harvey Morton
- *The Intentional Mindset* by Jane Frankel
- *Still Room for Humans* by Stan Schatt
- *Am I Doing This Right?* by Tony D. Thelen, Matthew C. Mitchell, and Jeffrey A. Kappen
- *Telling Your Story, Building Your Brand* by Henry Wong
- *Social Media Is About People* by Cassandra Bailey and Dana M. Schmidt
- *Pay Attention!* by Cassandra M. Bailey and Dana M. Schmidt
- *Remaining Relevant* by Karen Lawson
- *The Road to Champagne* by Alejandro Colindres Frañó

Concise and Applied Business Books

The Collection listed above is one of 30 business subject collections that Business Expert Press has grown to make BEP a premiere publisher of print and digital books. Our concise and applied books are for…

- Professionals and Practitioners
- Faculty who adopt our books for courses
- Librarians who know that BEP's Digital Libraries are a unique way to offer students ebooks to download, not restricted with any digital rights management
- Executive Training Course Leaders
- Business Seminar Organizers

Business Expert Press books are for anyone who needs to dig deeper on business ideas, goals, and solutions to everyday problems. Whether one print book, one ebook, or buying a digital library of 110 ebooks, we remain the affordable and smart way to be business smart. For more information, please visit www.businessexpertpress.com, or contact sales@businessexpertpress.com.

www.ingramcontent.com/pod-product-compliance
Lightning Source LLC
Chambersburg PA
CBHW061326220326
41599CB00026B/5054